FAMOUS JUDGES AND FAMOUS TRIALS

FAMOUS JUDGES AND FAMOUS TRIALS

BY

CHARLES KINGSTON

FRED B. ROTHMAN & CO.
Littleton, Colorado 80127

1988

Library of Congress Cataloging-in-Publication Data

Kingston, Charles.
Famous judges and famous trials.

Reprint. Originally published: New York : F.A. Stokes, 1923.
Includes index.
1. Judges--Great Britain--Biography. 2. Trials--Great Britain. I. Title.
KD620.K56 1988 347.41'014'0922 87-36177
344.107140922
ISBN 0-8377-2336-1 (alk. paper)

This reprinted edition does not contain nine portraits that were included in the original publication.

The paper used in this publication meets the minimum requirements of American National Standard for Information Sciences—Permanence of Paper for Printed Library Materials, ANSI Z39.48-1984.

FAMOUS JUDGES AND FAMOUS TRIALS

BY

CHARLES KINGSTON

NEW YORK

FREDERICK A. STOKES COMPANY

PUBLISHERS

PRINTED IN GREAT BRITAIN

PREFACE

My choice of twelve judges is necessarily an arbitrary one, and the only excuse I can offer is that each of them interests me in a special degree. The fact that I treat them purely as judges and not as authorities on church or state is an innovation, but when all is said and done Coleridge did not attain the position of Lord Chief Justice because he was an ardent churchman, and Cockburn is not remembered for his political speeches, but because he prosecuted Palmer and presided over many notable trials. I have not, of course, attempted to give anything like a complete account of all the celebrated trials with which the names of my twelve are indissolubly connected, but I hope that my selection will be found interesting. Judges are human enough to quarrel amongst themselves and their wit is sometimes sharpened by personal jealousies, but to the public they have ever presented a united front and justice has not suffered at their hands. When Lord Westbury was informed of the date fixed for the Tichborne trial he remarked, "I am glad it is coming on soon because it must lead to the exposure of at least one impostor." The reference was to Coleridge, whose incorrigible suavity irritated the ex-Lord Chancellor. But no harm is done by these fraternal differences. It is only when the public have cause to criticise the judges that their failings really matter. On the whole, however, there has been little reason for dissatisfaction, and if occasionally Parliament has been agitated by accusations of political partisanship against certain judges no one has ever been able to prove that the impartiality of the Bench has been affected.

CHARLES KINGSTON.

CONTENTS

CHAPTER VI

LORD CHIEF JUSTICE COLERIDGE

CHAPTER VII

LORD RUSSELL OF KILLOWEN

CHAPTER VIII

LORD ALVERSTONE

CHAPTER IX

LORD CHIEF JUSTICE COCKBURN

CHAPTER X

LORD CHIEF JUSTICE POLLOCK

CHAPTER XI

SIR SAMUEL MARTIN

PAGE

CHAPTER XII

LORD BRAMWELL

FAMOUS JUDGES AND FAMOUS TRIALS

CHAPTER I

Mr. Justice Grantham

When in 1886 the Lord Chancellor raised Mr. William Grantham, Q.C., M.P., to the Bench, he was severely criticised in certain quarters for giving high judicial office to a barrister who was mainly known as a political partisan, the critics maintaining that there were at least half a dozen men better qualified to fill the vacancy amongst the judges. Lord Halsbury, however, had the virtue of knowing his own mind, and he ignored the personal attacks and left it to his protégé to vindicate him. But Mr. Justice Grantham was of the Halsbury stamp, and his independence, fearlessness and brusqueness led to so many court "scenes" and condemnations in Press and Parliament that, while it cannot be said he was a failure, it must be admitted that he occasionally forgot the sound rule that a judge must not interfere with politics lest justice should suffer.

Sir William Grantham was born in 1835, was called to the Bar in his early twenties, entered Parliament in 1874, and became Q.C. in 1877. He remained in Parliament until he was appointed a judge, and his Parliamentary reputation was that of a big, strong man who was fond of dealing blows at his opponents and quite imperturbable when attacked in turn. In after years, when he was a veteran, Grantham remarked that he was sorry he had accepted a judgeship, as he believed he would have attained to Cabinet rank had he remained in Parliament. However, as we have seen, he went to the Bench, and those who knew him were quite prepared for some excitement when he started work as a judge. And they had not long to wait either.

It was not that he was a cantankerous person. In private life the judge was greatly loved. His manner was genial, generous, and hospitable. He was a typical country gentleman, fond of field sports, and a great believer in land. He inherited a goodly estate in Sussex from his father, and there during vacations he was the benevolent magnate. There was no more popular personage in the country, even when the papers were raging against his latest "judicial indiscretion."

For many years the judge was in the habit of riding from his house in Eaton Square to the Law Courts, and pedestrians, puzzled by the unusual sight of the distinguished-looking gentleman dressed like a country squire pulling up his horse in front of the Law Courts, wondered who he was, and generally believed that he was a witness from the country who was not aware of the fact that a horseman in the crowded Strand is a rarity. Very few realised that he was the judge who, a few minutes later, would preside over a court in the full panoply of office. He certainly brought a touch of the country into the vitiated atmosphere of the Law Courts and nobody could have been ungrateful for that.

Sir William Grantham was a judge from 1886 to the end of 1911, and he was busy from start to finish. When his fatal illness attacked him he was in the middle of a sensational action for libel brought by a South African millionaire—Sir J. B. Robinson—against a London journalist, and it must have caused the old judge acute mental distress to know that he was keeping his court waiting. He loved his work, and more than once, when really unwell, he insisted upon attending to his duties. On one occasion he was so ill that he could not speak, but he ignored his doctor's advice to go to bed, and when it came to summing-up he wrote out his charge and handed it to his marshal to read to the jury.

Once he was in a provincial city for the assizes, but on the morning he was to have addressed the grand jury he found himself unable to rise from his bed. He sent for the members of the grand jury, and when they had filed into his bedroom he delivered his charge there and then to them.

No time was wasted with Grantham. He could not contemplate idleness without a shudder. When it was suggested that he should retire—he became entitled to a full pension in 1901—he regarded the proposal with undisguised horror, and as there is no law to compel a judge to vacate his position, he remained on active service until the end.

Of all the remarkable trials over which he presided the most notable was that of George Chapman for the murder of three women by poisoning. This took place at the Old Bailey in March, 1903, and aroused enormous interest.

Chapman was an utterly unscrupulous scoundrel, who murdered women because he had no further use for them. Three times he "wooed" his victims, and, although already a married man, went through ceremonies of marriage with two of them, whilst the third and last victim, Maud Marsh, was persuaded to tell her parents that she had married him.

Chapman's real name was Klosowski, and he came from Poland, but, like so many aliens, he thought it better to take an English name, and so he went to bed one night as Klosowski and woke up next morning as "George Chapman." There was something more inviting about this name than his Polish one, as he speedily discovered.

It was in 1897 that he began his career as a poisoner. He had left his wife and was posing as a bachelor when he met Isabella Spink. The girl had a few pounds when she married him, but Chapman soon grew tired of her and decided to get rid of her. He therefore purchased some tartaric emetic from a chemist, and administered a few doses, and very shortly afterwards poor Isabella Spink was in her grave.

When it is remembered that this happened as recently as 1897 we must marvel that there was no inquest and that the murderer had not the slightest difficulty in securing a death certificate. But apparently antimony produces results which are similar to death from natural causes.

The murder of his second "wife" was on much the same lines, but Chapman gained more by her death, for she left sufficient money to enable him to take a public-house in the city of London. When he was a publican he had, of course, to employ a barmaid, and, as it happened, Maud Marsh was the successful applicant for the post.

He selected her because of her good looks, and his intention was to marry her, and when he got tired dispose of her in his usual way. Murder must have appeared to him to be one of the easiest of crimes. Apparently, a common pickpocket ran greater risks than he did, for had he not murdered two women with complete immunity?

Poor Maud Marsh, who was fascinated by the scoundrel, fell an easy victim to his wiles. She was delighted to be friendly with her employer, who appeared to be a rich man to her. He spoke of his wealth and of the money he had in the bank, and although for a time she resisted his temptations, she succumbed at last. But she had parents, most respectable persons, who were naturally anxious to see their daughter settled in life. They had no objection to her marrying a publican, but they would not hear of anything that was not straight and above board. The girl's mother, accordingly, kept an eye on things, and paid occasional visits to the public-house, and Chapman realised that if he wished to hoodwink Mrs. Marsh he must get her daughter to join him in deceiving her.

One morning Mrs. Marsh arrived at the public-house to find the pathway strewn with confetti. She was delighted, for she had been troubled by certain doubts as to her daughter's position. Now all seemed perfectly straight. Her first question was to ask where the ceremony had taken place. Maud replied vaguely that it had been performed according to the rites of the Roman Catholic Church, and in a private room. Mrs. Marsh, not being a Catholic, accepted the information, though she wondered why they had not been married in a church.

However, her daughter must have her marriage lines, so all was well. When she asked to see the latter a laughing reply was made, and then she was taken into the dining-room, where a feast was spread, and during the ensuing merriment her suspicions were dissipated, and she returned home thankful that Maud was respectably married to a well-to-do man.

It was, of course, only a sham, and Maud Marsh had acted as her employer had ordered her to do. She had sprinkled the confetti before the public-house to deceive her mother—a strange and very pathetic incident in view of subsequent events. I can imagine the girl wishing that the confetti-sprinkling was not a mockery, for she loved Chapman in her own queer way.

The bogus marriage had one important effect on Maud Marsh's position. It now became necessary that their neighbours should accept them as man and wife, and to insure this Chapman had to treat her as his wife. She, therefore, ceased to be his barmaid, as she was above that now. "Mrs. Chapman" was, in fact, to become what she considered a lady—to have her own servant, and to cease to have any concern with the rough work of the establishment. It was a life that appealed to the girl, and she gladly welcomed the appearance of a new barmaid, a pretty girl, who had been engaged by Chapman for the very same reason that had led to Maud Marsh's introduction to his public-house.

What followed can be readily surmised. Chapman became fond of the new barmaid and neglected his "wife." He soon had no further interest in the girl who had lied to her mother for him and who had forsaken all her friends and relations in order to be his paramour. He left Maud Marsh to dawdle away her time while he paid court to the barmaid, and he brought matters to a head when he asked the girl to elope with him to Canada. The barmaid was horrified at the idea. She was under the impression that Chapman and Maud Marsh were man and wife, and she instantly gave the poisoner a month's notice.

Meanwhile, however, Chapman had resolved on Maud's death. She was in his way. He wanted to trick the barmaid into "marrying" him, and it was necessary to remove his putative wife. He, therefore, started to poison Maud, and although a hospital nurse was called in when her illness began to get critical, Chapman continued to administer antimony. He would hardly allow the nurse to do anything, and even when injection had to be resorted to he did it himself.

Chapman was so free from care that while he knew his "wife" was doomed he entertained friends in his billiard-room. The night before her death it was noticed that he played billiards better than ever, and his geniality and generosity to customers betokened a mind exulting in good news or in the expectation of it.

But the third time paid for all. The doctor who was attending Maud Marsh was greatly puzzled by the symptoms. He recalled the fact that once before when she had suffered in the same way and had been removed to hospital she had recovered. Now she was under her "husband's" care, and, instead of getting better, she was growing rapidly worse. Unhappily for the victim it was too late to save her, but when she died the doctor refused a certificate, and the body was removed to the mortuary for an inquest to be held on it. Even now Chapman anticipated no danger. He must have thought that the doctors would not suspect poison, or, if they did, would be unable to discover traces of it. He made not the slightest attempt to get away, and every day was to be found in his public-house, going about his ordinary duties.

He was actually arrested with a billiard-cue in his hand! It is incredible that he did not realise that arrest was inevitable from the moment the doctor had refused to issue a death certificate.

It is a commonplace to say that the most callous murderers are the greatest cowards. It was so in the case of George Chapman. When he appeared before Mr. Justice Grantham at the Old Bailey he was almost paralysed by terror. Dully he listened to the prosecution, conducted by Sir Edward Carson, K.C., M.P., then Solicitor-General and now a Life Peer and a Lord of Appeal. His own counsel was the late Mr. George Elliott, K.C., who must have known that he was fighting a hopeless battle. Chapman's fright rendered him incapable of being of the slightest use to his defenders, and Mr. Elliott, who could call no evidence on behalf of his client, relied upon a clever speech, which, however, did not damage the case for the Crown. He could only ask the jury to hesitate before they returned a verdict of guilty because there was no motive for the murders. But, as Sir Edward Carson pointed out, there was a motive, and it was lust.

Mr. Justice Grantham, when passing sentence, dwelt with emphasis and relief on the fact that the prisoner was not an Englishman. The judge, who was the embodiment of frankness and who hated anything underhand or mean, was particularly scathing as he addressed the trembling wretch. Chapman, who could play billiards whilst his victim was dying in agony, had to be assisted from the dock, and he died a coward's death as well as a murderer's when the official hangman performed his duty.

It must be remembered that it was one of Sir William's " whims " that led to the discovery of one of the greatest miscarriages of justice on record. He was presiding at the Old Bailey, and a man stood in the dock charged with swindling certain women. Counsel had been heard on either side, and the jury had returned to court with a verdict of guilty. Nothing remained but to pass sentence, and his lordship had already scribbled on the pad before him the number of years he had decided to inflict on the convict, when, suddenly, he glanced at the prisoner. Then, to the surprise of everybody in court, he said, " I will postpone sentence until next sessions. In the meantime the police will make further inquiries into the convict's antecedents."

It was a decision which became historic, for the man in the dock was Adolf Beck, and between those fateful sessions Chief-Inspector John Kane, of New Scotland Yard, solved the great mystery, and proved that Adolf Beck had suffered for another man's sins.

A commission was appointed to inquire into the strange affair, and eventually Beck was paid five thousand pounds as compensation for the tortures he had suffered when undergoing the seven years' penal servitude to which he had been sentenced in 1896, the occasion of his first conviction for a crime of which he was completely innocent. Grantham was very proud of his acumen in this case, and he wrote to Beck—who did not survive his vindication for long—congratulating him on his triumph over a cruel fate.

The judge admitted that at the time of the trial he was almost convinced that Beck was guilty, but that when the foreman of the jury had spoken and he had observed the anguish on the face of the prisoner he became doubtful, and decided to postpone passing sentence. It was very lucky for Beck that he did so, for if the convict had passed into penal servitude a second time he would never have had his innocence proved.

The trial of Walter Turner for the murder of Barbara Waterhouse, a child only five years of age, in 1891, was one of the first to attract public attention to Mr. Justice Grantham's methods. It was a sordid affair, but at the same time there were peculiarities about it, and it was remembered in Leeds and neighbourhood for many years.

Horsforth is a village within five miles of Leeds, and there, in June, 1891, the two families concerned in the case lived close to one another. Turner was a weaver, who was separated from his wife, and his mother kept house for him. One night Mrs. Turner, the widow, was horrified to find in the coal-shed the mutilated body of a little girl. It should be mentioned that Mrs. Turner had been away for a couple of days, and during that time her son had been the sole occupant of the cottage. She asked him at once for an explanation, and he told her a strange story.

He said that he had been drinking with a strange man in a public-house and that the stranger had accompanied him home, bringing with him a child whom he described as his daughter. After further drinking in the house, Walter Turner went on, all three had retired to rest, Turner sleeping soundly until the morning. When he awoke he found that the man had disappeared, but that he had first murdered the little girl. In a state of terror Turner had then wrapped the body in a shawl and had taken it to the coal-shed, and now he implored his mother to help him out of his dilemma.

Mrs. Turner was naturally anxious to believe her son to be incapable of such a brutal murder, but she could not come to a decision without advice. She went, therefore, to some neighbours who were relatives and told her story, and they advised her to put the whole affair in the hands of the police. This was not to Mrs. Turner's liking, however, and she rejected it, and she eventually took the body, wrapped in the shawl as it was, and, escorted by her son, left it after dark outside Leeds Town Hall. They got back to Horsforth at one in the morning exhausted by the strain of that pilgrimage of horror.

The body was found by two policemen, and as it was clearly a case of murder, the entire detective force concentrated on the attempt to find the criminal. Their energies were soon rewarded.

A neighbour who had been consulted by Mrs. Turner read of the discovery in the papers and in conjunction with her husband she sent an anonymous letter to the inspector in charge at Horsforth police station. It was simply a statement to the effect that if he charged "Walter Lewis Turner, of Back Lane, Horsforth," he would "convict himself at once."

Strangely enough this communication was

not acted upon at once. Anonymous letters have played their part in sensational crimes—one led to the arrest of Dr. Pritchard—but in Turner's case it was his mother's statement at the Leeds Detective Office that solved the brief mystery.

The old woman must have had an extraordinary belief in her son's truthfulness, for with astonishing *naiveté* she retold the whole amazing story to the police, and, although surprised when she was detained, expressed her belief that an investigation would clear both their characters. Turner was immediately arrested, and at the assizes both were tried by Mr. Justice Grantham and a jury.

It was a trial full of incidents, but the judge was the chief object of interest to the crowded court. The personality of the two prisoners faded away before the strong, forceful character on the Bench. Taking command of the case in no uncertain manner, he first had the mother tried and convicted, and an audible "Oh!" of amazement went through the audience when he passed sentence of twenty years' penal servitude. It was in the circumstances a brutal punishment. A mother could not be expected to denounce her own son with that promptness which anybody else would be expected to show. Then, again, Mrs. Turner had given her evidence against her son with the obvious desire to get at the truth.

Mr. Justice Grantham proceeded calmly with the trial of the murderer. It was, of course, a formality. Not only was Turner unable to produce any evidence of the existence of the man with whom he had said he had spent the night in various public-houses and whom he charged with the crime, but the prosecution brought forward witnesses who swore that they had seen the prisoner on the night in question, and he had then been quite alone. The only possible verdict was guilty, and sentence of death ensued.

So great was the public rancour against Turner that when Sir William Grantham left the court he was cheered by the crowd. Doubtless their cheers had as much effect upon him as the hisses he encountered in another provincial city when his decisions met with the disapproval of the majority. It was the Grantham way to appear grim and hard, and yet he was very emotional. It is a fact that when he was summoned for a trivial, technical offence against the building laws and was fined a few shillings by the magistrates he shed tears!

But to return to the Turner trial. With the passing of sentence on both convicts it was thought that the case was over so far as Mr. Justice Grantham was concerned, but that was not to be so. The next day the same judge was to take other trials, but, before he began the business of the day, he called before him the two neighbours, husband and wife, whom Mrs. Turner had consulted. The judge congratulated them on their public-spirited performance in writing that anonymous letter to the police, and as a reward, he informed them, he had decided to reduce the sentence of their relative, Mrs. Turner, from twenty years to twelve months! The reduction was equally as startling as the original sentence, but that was the Grantham way.

A breach of promise case which Mr. Grantham heard had a sequel in a trial for perjury at the Old Bailey. It was a curious affair from first to last, and the person most concerned was a rather remarkable woman with a dubious record.

Mrs. Sophia Annie Watson, who brought the action, told the judge and jury that when she was serving a term of three years' penal servitude she made the acquaintance of the defendant, Major-General Fitzhugh. The general was one of the visiting justices, and, it was alleged by Mrs. Watson, he had offered to marry her when she was free again. It was obviously a very good match for the lady, for apart from his military rank, the general was a county magnate, and he was not a poor man. Mrs. Watson was anxious to become Mrs. Fitzhugh, and when the general resented her attentions on her release she entered the action, claiming damages to the extent of ten thousand pounds.

Although this was a civil action, the fair plaintiff appeared in the custody of a wardress, having had the bad luck to be re-arrested for failing, as a convict out on licence, to report her movements to the police, but the presence of the gaoler did not affect her in the slightest, and she conducted her case with considerable skill and tremendous vivacity. More than once she met the brusque comments and interjections of the judge with a cleverness that elicited admiration, but she did not succeed in convincing the jury that a retired general had actually proposed marriage to a woman who had been convicted more than once of fraud. They found for the defendant, and Mrs. Watson left the court in the society of the wardress. Later on another judge tried her at the Old Bailey for perjury committed at the hearing of the breach of promise case, and on this occasion she scored a personal triumph, for the jury disagreed! A second time, however, she faced the jury, and her fate was different. She was convicted, and sent to penal servitude for four years.

One of the fiercest controversies the judge was involved in arose out of a charge of manslaughter. When Sir William was informed that the accused had been undoubtedly intoxicated when he committed the crime, he remarked, "Publicans who supply drunken men with liquor should be charged with them, unless they can prove that the accused were sober when they left their premises." The statement sent the publicans into a frenzy, and in press and public they did their best to retaliate. Mr. Justice Grantham was quite unperturbed, for he offended again when another prisoner pleaded drunkenness as an excuse by blandly inquiring why the publican who had supplied him with drink was not by his side in the dock.

This sort of thing incensed "the trade," and they showered letters of protest upon his lordship. His only comment was, "I am in the habit of receiving letters from persons of unsound mind, and I always fling them into the waste-paper basket."

The fraternity of bookmakers also came in for his censure.

"Never take a cheque from a bookmaker," he advised a suitor, and again he was subjected to much abuse. Bookmakers must be wishing now that they had never accepted cheques from their clients.

But this was nothing to his experience as an election judge, and his undisguised partisanship led to the question of his fitness to remain a judge being brought up in Parliament time after time, and a strong effort was made to induce him to resign. But he stuck to his post, and he continued to work until he was in his seventy-seventh year. Even then it was only death that removed the fearless judge from his position.

Those who only knew Sir William Grantham in his public capacity can hardly understand his popularity in private life. He was a human paradox, and he succeeded in escaping from that isolation which a seat on the Bench usually entails by entering into the pursuits and the pleasures of the country he loved and where he was really seen at his best.

CHAPTER II

Lord Blackburn

Had Lord Blackburn depended on his reputation with "the man in the street," he would never have reached the Bench, for after twenty years at the Bar he was practically unknown outside professional circles. However, Lord Campbell thought highly of his friend's abilities, and when he had the opportunity he appointed Blackburn a judge, and for thirty-seven years the country had the benefit of his services.

Those who remember Lord Blackburn—as he subsequently became—recall a strong face and a determined expression, a harsh voice that revealed his Scottish birth, a nervous horror of female witnesses, and a half-ironic consciousness of the intellectual inferiority of the barristers who practised before him. He could be kind, but in a brusque way, as if ashamed of displaying such a weakness, and he was dignified and severe and impatient with bores.

His duties involved him in several murder trials, which must have been utterly distasteful to one whose tastes were scholarly. But he never shrank from the uncongenial, though when he was promoted to the highest court in the land, the House of Lords, he must have regarded that august place as a place of refuge from the vulgarities of criminal courts.

The most remarkable trial over which Mr.

Justice Blackburn presided was that of a German, Johann Carl Franz, who was charged at the Croydon Assizes in 1861 with the murder of Mrs. Martha Halliday. The case against the accused was a very strong one, and when counsel for the prosecution — Serjeant Ballantine— opened the proceedings, he had not spoken for half an hour before everybody in court, with one or two exceptions, felt that the prisoner was doomed. Martha Halliday's murder was a most cruel and wanton crime. She was the wife of the parish clerk of Kingswood, near Reigate, and when the rector was away she was engaged to look after the rectory.

In June, 1861, the rector took his family and all his servants to his father-in-law's place at Dorking, and the parish clerk's wife, as usual, was called upon to take charge of the deserted house. On Sundays, however, the rector had to take the usual services, and then he slept at the rectory, going back to Dorking on the Monday morning. This programme was carried out on the day before the murder, and on Monday evening the parish clerk accompanied his wife to the rectory, saw her safely in and then went home again, as their own house could not be left unoccupied.

This was the state of affairs on Monday evening. In the early hours of the morning someone broke into the rectory, seized Mrs. Halliday—she was fifty-five—bound and gagged her, and proceeded to explore the house, but, becoming alarmed, decamped without taking anything.

The following morning, Mr. Halliday called for his wife, and, to his surprise, he found the front door open. Entering at once he called her by name, but there was no response, and he instantly rushed up the stairs to her room.

A few moments later he was kneeling beside his wife's corpse. She was bound hand and foot with hempen cord, a handkerchief was tied over her face, and a sock had been thrust into her mouth. She had been dead for at least six hours.

When the police were summoned and the body of the murdered woman had been removed an important discovery was made, and one which apparently solved the mystery at once. This was a bundle of papers, several of which related to a German of the name of Johann Carl Franz. They were, in fact, identity papers—passport, birth and baptism certificates—and they also contained a comprehensive description of the person to whom they had been issued by the German authorities, and were, of course, entirely written in the Teuton language.

A few documents not bearing Franz's name were included. These were an application to Madame Tietjens, the famous operatic artiste, for financial help, signed "Adolphe Krohn"; a letter from the latter undertaking to pay the cost of her fellow-countryman's return to Germany, and a list of prominent residents in London, obviously the work of a begging-letter writer of German nationality.

The clues were, therefore, many and conclusive, and the authorities and the public decided that Johann Carl Franz was the murderer, and that in his hurry to get away upon being alarmed he had dropped his papers of identification. That a German had done the crime was plain, and during the succeeding days this was confirmed by several people who were able to prove that on the Sunday before the murder two foreigners, Germans, had appeared in Reigate and had as suddenly disappeared about the time that the murder had been committed.

About three weeks later a German was arrested in the East End of London on a charge of stealing a few coppers from a fellow-lodger in one of the awful "doss-houses" near the docks. He was taken to the police station and questioned, when a detective expressed the opinion that Salzmann, as the prisoner called himself, was in reality Franz, one of the men wanted for the Kingswood murder. Further inquiries established the truth of this, and, after the usual magisterial investigation, Franz, who soon admitted his identity, was committed for trial, and at the Croydon Assizes on August 6th, Mr. Justice Blackburn heard the case.

Serjeant Ballantine's speech for the prosecution and the evidence of the Crown witnesses seemed to leave the prisoner without any defence. The accused had recognised his identification papers, though he had remarked that a testimonial from a railway guard which he prized highly was missing.

In addition to this damning admission the police, when searching the room in which Franz had lodged in Whitechapel, found a woollen shirt tied up with a piece of hempen string of the same manufacture as that which had been used to bind Mrs. Halliday. This fact alone seemed proof positive that the prisoner had taken part in the murder. The maker of the hempen cord was called, and he proved that there were peculiarities about it which made it quite distinct from any other string manufactured in this country, and he also demonstrated that the hempen cord which had bound Mrs. Halliday and the piece which had been found in Franz's lodgings had come from his factory. He added that there was a shop in Reigate which he supplied regularly with this string.

But the defence met all this with some equally remarkable evidence. Mr. Denman, Q.C., afterwards a judge, told Franz's story as to how he lost his identification papers. He said that the prisoner had been robbed by two fellow-countrymen a long way from Kingswood. Franz, on his arrest, had sworn that he had never been in Reigate in his life.

Clearly counsel for the defence wished to persuade the jury that if the police could find Adolphe Krohn, whose begging letter to Madame Tietjens had been found with Franz's papers, and his companion, whose name, according to the accused, was Wilhelm Gerstenberg, they would have the actual murderers of Martha Halliday. But even if this uncorroborated story was accepted it did not explain the coincidence of the hempen string.

Certainly the witnesses who had come forward to identify Franz as one of the men seen in Reigate on the Sunday before the murder had picked him out at the police station after failing at first to recognise him, and when they did, as the police had to admit, their manner of doing so was unsatisfactory. Of course, while this was the first weakness in the case for the prosecution, it was undoubtedly strengthened by the fact that hempen string had been found in the prisoner's possession.

Mr. Denman undertook to explain away the coincidence. The prosecution had called as a witness the solicitor who was acting for the man in the dock, and Mr. Denman proceeded to cross-examine him at length about the string. Franz had declared that he had picked it up outside a tobacconist's shop in the Whitechapel Road, and, of course, every one had smiled at this. But his counsel was able to extract from the witness the astonishing information that the place where this peculiar hempen string was manufactured was only a minute's walk from the tobacconist's shop Franz had named, and that balls of the string were to be found all over the district. There was, therefore, nothing remarkable in the German's story as to how he had obtained it.

Another point in the prisoner's favour was the discovery by a couple of tramps of a book, which proved to be a diary which Franz had kept. It contained entries relating to his travels over England, and it terminated with an account of his doings at Leek on the date he had said he had been robbed by his fellow-countrymen. The book was found at Northampton, and it confirmed his account of his loss of the all-important identification papers.

By itself this would have meant little, but taken in conjunction with other evidence it told considerably in his favour. That Madame Tietjens should swear in the witness-box that Franz was not the Adolphe Krohn who had appealed to her for help counted for nothing, as the theory of the prosecution was that Krohn and Franz had committed the murder between them.

When the jury retired, ten out of the twelve, it was afterwards reported, had made up their minds that the accused was guilty.

Yet no one was surprised that they should take some hours to arrive at a verdict. It was a most difficult case, all the more so because a verdict of guilty could not be revised. The brutal murder had aroused the animosity of the country against Franz, and if he were convicted there could be no hope of a reprieve. The jury had, therefore, to guard against making an error which would be irretrievable.

Mr. Justice Blackburn, who conducted the proceedings with scrupulous impartiality, gave the prisoner the benefit of all the points adduced in his favour, going over them carefully and emphasising their strength as well as their weakness. It was, I think, this summing-up that caused the majority of the members of the jury to reconsider their opinion and return a verdict of not guilty.

In no other country would Franz have been acquitted, for nowhere else would he have been tried by so impartial a judge and jury. There was, of course, a large section of the public which disagreed with the verdict, animated by the chivalry which is always aroused by the murder of a defenceless woman. But, even if Franz was guilty, there was not sufficient evidence to justify conviction. The jury took the judge's broad hint not to run the risk of assisting in a judicial murder, and they set the German free.

At the Old Bailey on December 16th, 1863, Mr. Justice Blackburn had before him a murderer with a remarkable personality, and the curious scene was witnessed of the learned judge trying to persuade a prisoner to offer some sort of defence. He did not succeed, however, and the accused was sentenced to death.

It was a sordid, miserable affair altogether, this story of how a woman's jealousy led to her murder at the hands of the man who called himself her husband.

The setting for the tragedy was a squalid tenement house in the Waterloo Road, which fifty years ago was even worse than it is now. Samuel Wright was a bricklayer who came from the country to seek work in London, and when he met Maria Green, a domestic servant out of employment, he suggested that they should live together as man and wife. This was agreeable to Maria, and a room in the Waterloo Road was taken. But if she had not her "marriage lines," Maria Green insisted upon regarding Wright as her husband, and would not tolerate his attentions to the "ladies" of the neighbourhood. The woman was of an intensely jealous disposition. and she wearied Wright with nagging. He was a good-humoured, quiet man, who liked to chaff his lady friends, but he gave Maria no real cause for offence. However, she hotly resented her "husband's" popularity, and she sought to "reform" him by constantly forcing quarrels on him.

No one actually witnessed the murder, but when Wright had taken the life of the woman who had rendered him miserable, he went down to the basement kitchen and waited there until the police came and arrested him. He confessed immediately, and then seemed to forget the subject, refusing to discuss it or comment on it in any way.

The murder was committed on December 13th, and three days later Wright was in the dock at the Old Bailey. He had refused to defend himself at the police court, and had, therefore, been committed, and, as the sessions were on, he found himself before Mr. Justice Blackburn three days after the murder. This is a record which can never be equalled, as, owing to the criticism it caused, a rule was introduced postponing the trial of any accused person committed during the sittings at the Old Bailey to the following sessions.

The judge did not wish the accused to plead guilty, and he urged him to defend himself, but Wright merely answered that he had committed the crime, and that the sooner it was all over the better. Of course, after that, Mr. Justice Blackburn could only do his duty and sentence him to death, and Wright went from the dock quite unperturbed. He never gave the slightest trouble to the authorities, and took very little interest, if any, in the efforts that were made to obtain a reprieve.

The Home Secretary had created a precedent by reprieving George Victor Townley, an educated man with influential parents, and it was felt by the working classes that a distinction was being made between rich and poor, and that Townley had been saved from the hangman only because he was a member of a good family. But the Home Secretary did not flinch from his obvious duty when the judge who had tried Wright expressed the opinion that the convict was quite sane and that he was fully conscious of the enormity of his crime. The law, therefore, took its course, and Samuel Wright was executed.

Many of the judges who were on the Bench in the 'sixties came into contact with Fenian agitators, and Blackburn took a memorable part in the suppression of the crimes committed by those terrorists. He was the judge who sentenced to death the murderers Allen, Larkin, and Gould, who called himself O'Brien because he thought an English name did not suit an Irish "patriot."

It is nearly sixty years since the Manchester police took into custody two suspicious-looking men, who proved to be leaders of a dangerous gang of Irish-American political fanatics. That it was a very important capture became evident by the dismay the arrests caused in the ranks of the agitators, but the police were hardly prepared for what followed. The friends of the prisoners decided to rescue them, and, in order to leave nothing to chance, about sixty of them, armed with revolvers, attacked the prison van as it approached the railway arch in Hyde Road. The horses were shot, and only the bad marksmanship of the attackers saved the driver and his two comrades from a similar fate.

The moment the van was brought to a standstill it was surrounded by the gang, twenty of whom kept the police at bay whilst certain of their friends proceeded to rescue the prisoners. They succeeded in smashing the lock of the door, but each prisoner was locked up in a separate compartment, the keys of which were in the possession of Sergeant Brett, the officer in charge. The leader of the Fenians demanded them from him. To this request the courageous officer returned an emphatic refusal, adding that it was his duty to keep the prisoners in custody.

The rioters were six to one as they faced the gallant sergeant, and they could easily have overpowered him and taken the keys from him, but the mob was out for blood, and as Allen was only a few paces from Brett he could hardly miss him. He raised his revolver and deliberately shot the sergeant dead.

It was a cowardly, cruel murder, but the

ruffian, maddened by blood, thought of nothing but the release of the prisoners, and soon afterwards all those in the van were free, including some boys and women who were under remand for minor offences.

The authorities could not, of course, give in to the murderers, and Manchester and district were scoured for the criminals. It was not long before the leaders were lodged in gaol, and when they were committed for trial a special commission of two judges, Mellor and Blackburn, was sent down to Manchester to try them.

Allen, Larkin, and Gould were convicted and executed publicly, and two of their fellow-prisoners were released by the Home Secretary's orders. Before the executions friends of the condemned made strenuous efforts to secure a reprieve, and they did not improve their chances by uttering threats against judges, counsel, and Cabinet Ministers. One excited partisan called at the Home Office, and, when refused an interview, forced his way into the Home Secretary's office. But in the midst of an harangue, which was chiefly directed against the judges who had presided at the trial, he was bundled out, and henceforth oblivion claimed him.

Swinburne passionately protested in verse and lived to regret his outburst, and hordes of minor poets sang in the hope that the convicts would be unhung.

Mr. Justice Blackburn was pestered with anonymous letters of praise and abuse, the latter greatly predominating. His life was threatened by illiterate correspondents, who seemed to have very peculiar ideas as to his powers. They thought that because he had sentenced the men to death he could revoke the order for their execution. He was accused of being a political partisan who had condemned the men not because they were murderers, but because they were of an opposite school of political thought. As Blackburn had never been in Parliament and had never taken part in politics the charge was absurd; indeed, the Government could not have selected a better judge for a trial of this nature. But the excitement created by the Manchester affray finds an echo in certain parts of Ireland to-day, where the three men are styled the "Manchester Martyrs" and honoured with a yearly celebration.

In spite of the threats against the judges and others no one was injured by the friends of the "martyrs," and Blackburn lived to a good old age and never lost his reputation for fairness. He and his colleagues were the factors which crushed the Fenian conspirators and restored law and order in places where previously one had been ignored and the other unknown.

A very mysterious case of attempted murder came before him at the Old Bailey, in which a father was the accused, and his son the alleged victim. Baron de Vidil was an intimate friend of the Orleans family, which had been exiled from France by the success of Napoleon III in achieving the position of Emperor of the French. The baron and his son were on good terms, and if now and then they fell out it was over something trivial, and they were soon friends again. However, one morning in June father and son were out riding together in a lane in the vicinity of Twickenham, where Orleans House, the headquarters of the exiled royalties, was situated. They chatted on various topics until they came to a very secluded part of the lane, and then the baron allowed his son to ride on a little way in front. The youth—he was only nineteen—suspecting nothing, rode on, and a moment later was startled by a fearful blow on his head. Turning, he caught a glimpse of his father's face, his eyes gleaming with murderous hatred, whilst his right hand held a heavily loaded hunting crop.

Before the young man could escape, the baron inflicted several more blows upon him, and when at last the youth threw himself from his saddle he was covered with blood. Just then am an and a woman appeared in the lane, and to them young Vidil appealed for protection. His father, however, was finished with him, for, realising his own danger, he rode post haste to the railway station and went to Paris.

The man and woman who had tended young Vidil reported the matter to the police, and although the victim would not prosecute, it was decided to bring the baron back from Paris to stand his trial. At this time England was crowded with political refugees, and many of them seemed unable to understand that crimes of violence were heavily punished in Great Britain. It took a great deal to persuade the foreign colony, for example, that duelling was a criminal offence.

The baron was arrested in Paris, and Napoleon III, who had no liking for the friends of the Orleans family, ordered him to be handed over to the English detectives, and he was taken to London and put in the dock at the Old Bailey.

But a difficulty arose at this stage of the proceedings. Baron de Vidil might have tried to murder his son, but that son was not going to give evidence against him. He absolutely declined to be a party to the prosecution, and he neither affirmed nor denied the sensational rumours that arose out of the incident.

What had caused Baron de Vidil to hate his son and wish to murder him? Had the two quarrelled about money matters, or had the older man discovered that the younger was betraying Orleanist secrets to the emissaries of Napoleon III. It was known that the French emperor was keeping a strict watch on his political opponents in England, and that French secret service men swarmed in the neighbourhood of Twickenham, where they tried to extract secrets from servants, shopkeepers, and other local residents.

On the other hand, some one declared that the son had found that his father was a traitor, and that it was to save himself that the baron had attempted to silence for ever the man who could have denounced him to the head of the Bourbons. French exiles in England had their own way of "removing" traitors to the cause, and if Baron de Vidil, or any one else in the Orleans camp, conveyed information to the enemy—in this case Napoleon III—he would have met with short shrift at the hands of his betrayed comrades.

These were the rumours arising out of the trial at the Old Bailey, and it was expected that it would result in revelations that would astonish both the French and the British. But young Vidil kept his own counsel, and his tenderness towards his father prevented any other charge but that of unlawful wounding being brought against him. He was convicted on the evidence of the witnesses, who had seen the younger man stagger towards them covered with blood, and a short term of imprisonment was inflicted.

It was the opinion of the celebrated barrister, Serjeant Ballantine, who defended the accused, that the baron was wholly in the wrong, and that he had a bad reputation amongst his fellow exiles. Efforts were made after the trial to obtain a clue to the mystery, but the son was not to be tempted or tricked into making a disclosure, and nothing more ever came of the matter.

When the free and independent electors of Great Britain were upset by the laws against bribery and corruption at elections, it took them quite a long time to understand that the laws must be obeyed, and consequently there were many election petitions, and many aspiring politicians of wealth and enterprise were declared unseated. Mr. Justice Blackburn heard many of these petitions, and they would have suited him better than criminal trials had it not been for the presence of fashionably dressed ladies, who swarmed all over the court and even invaded the Bench. The judge was not a ladies' man, and once he was placed in an extremely undignified position by a lady, all lace and flounces, stumbling over his legs as she was passing him on the Bench, and enveloping him for a few moments in her finery. Then the well-known Blackburn voice, harsh and Scottish, was heard protesting against the indignity, but, of course, he did nothing beyond expressing his annoyance.

It was different with a Surrey High Sheriff, who objected to the judge ordering a certain portion of the Croydon Court to be closed to the public. The sheriff issued a placard declaring the judge's order to be illegal, and Blackburn retaliated by fining him five hundred pounds for contempt of court.

In 1876 Blackburn was given a peerage, and in 1886 he retired from the administration of justice, though he filled in his time by serving on Royal Commissions and writing about the law. He was a famous Scotsman, who found honour in England as well as in his own country, and when he died in 1896 the nation lost a great jurist.

CHAPTER III

Mr. Justice Stephen

There is generally at least one judge on the Bench whose actions provoke criticism and who, consequently, becomes better known to the public than colleagues of greater eminence. A touch of independence, temper, or a determination to get his own way may be the cause, and if he succeeds he is called a "strong judge." If he does not, his memory merely revives old and worn-out controversies.

Sir James Fitzjames Stephen was a man of very decided views, strong-minded, given to expressing his opinions without fear or favour, a hater of cruelty, and constitutionally incapable of waxing sentimental over the woes of convicted wife-beaters.

He was physically a big man, with the face of a statesman and a crusty demeanour which was mainly pose. But there was too much of "an eye for an eye and a tooth for a tooth" in his judicial utterances to please everybody, and he was often sharply criticised. He was, however, not the sort of person to be moved by clamour, and he never showed the "white feather."

The son of an Under-Secretary of State for the Colonies, Stephen was born in 1829, educated at Eton and Cambridge, and called to the Bar in 1854. It must be recorded that he made no great stir as a barrister. Perhaps he was too good a journalist. Briefs were scarce, but Stephen soon gained a reputation as a brilliant writer on political and legal subjects, and he contributed hundreds of articles to *The Spectator*, *The Saturday Review*, *The Pall Mall Gazette*, and the principal reviews. The style of the journalist was terse, vivid, and trenchant. He knew his own mind, and said what he thought, and he engaged in combat with many intellectual giants, a notable encounter being with the philosopher, John Stuart Mill.

Stephen was not, however, satisfied with literary success. He wanted to earn fame and fortune as a barrister, and while his relations were in a position to help him they could not bring him that steady volume of business which paves the way to the Bench. Solicitors had reasonable grounds for supposing that Stephen was more suited to be a professor than an advocate, and they showered their briefs upon counsel not so eminent in the literary world.

He was one of the numerous barristers, however, who were consulted during the excitement caused by the now almost forgotten Eyre case. In its day it created many sensations, and it was responsible for the ending of numerous friendships.

The origin of it all was a rebellion in Jamaica in the early 'sixties of the last century. The negroes, resenting an attempt to arrest a convicted murderer, raised the standard of revolt, and as they numbered over four hundred thousand and the white population was less than thirteen thousand, it seemed as though the rebels must have their own way. They murdered and pillaged and destroyed until Governor Eyre, realising that stern measures must be adopted, flung himself and his handful of troops into the fray and overcame the rebellion. Dire punishments were meted out. Murderers were executed ; flogging was resorted to.

Matters came to a head when a half-caste of the name of Gordon was tried and executed for encouraging the rebels.

Then in far-away England attacks began to be made on Eyre. It was said that he had used unnecessary violence, and that Gordon had been convicted without justification. The critics of Eyre formed a committee which was powerful and influential enough to induce the Government to send out a commission of inquiry. The report of this body was virtually a severe censure of the governor, who was ordered to return to England.

But the Jamaica Committee did not intend to allow Governor Eyre to get off with a mere official reprimand, and in 1867, two years after the trial of Gordon, when the two officers who had held the court martial—Colonel Nelson and Lieutenant Brand, R.N.—arrived in London, the committee obtained warrants from Sir Thomas Henry, the Bow Street magistrate, charging them with the murder of Gordon.

They were committed for trial, but at the Old Bailey the grand jury threw out the bill. This was a bitter disappointment for the committee, the chairman of which was John Stuart Mill, and they tried to have Eyre placed in the dock.

Certain magistrates having refused to grant warrants on a charge of murder—Eyre had, of course, ordered Nelson and Brand to try Gordon—the committee succeeded in having him sent for trial on the ground that in his capacity as governor he had been oppressive. However, the grand jury threw out the bill, and Eyre was not troubled again with a criminal prosecution.

In 1869 an action was brought against him by one of the rebels, who declared that he had been beaten and imprisoned illegally, but as an act of indemnity had been passed by Parliament the ex-governor had only to plead it to secure a verdict in his favour.

The narrative makes rather tame reading to-day, but in the 'sixties families were divided over Eyre's merits and demerits. While the Jamaica committee was formed to prosecute him, another, even more influential, came into existence to defend him. He was given a banquet in England by his admirers when his enemies were denouncing him as a tyrant and a murderer. On the other hand, his friends maintained that he had saved the prestige of the white race, and that in the circumstances he was to be commended and not blamed.

The controversy lasted some years, but Eyre's supporters were strong enough to influence the Government to pay all the costs legally incurred by him. Stephen would have appeared for the defence had the charge of murder gone to trial. As it was he took considerable share of the hard work entailed by the preparation of the accused's case, though, of course, in open court leading counsel would have kept Stephen in the background.

At the age of forty, and a year after he had become Queen's Counsel, Stephen accepted the position of legal member of the Council in India, and for two and a half years he was away from England, spending that term mainly in codifying the Indian laws.

It was congenial work, but Stephen was not sorry to return to England, and he immediately made an attempt to enter Parliament, standing for Dundee in 1873 as a supporter of Mr. Gladstone's policy. He was not elected, however, and had to satisfy his ambitions with the post of Professor of Common Law at the Inns of Court. The appointment was not sought by him, but in reality it was the cause of his elevation to the Bench, for it led to undertaking certain important legal literary work for the Attorney-General, who promised that the first suitable vacancy amongst the judges should be given to him. The promise was kept, and in 1879 Stephen was created a Judge of the Queen's Bench.

He was unaffectedly pleased at his promotion. To a man of his temperament the struggle at the Bar had been distasteful. He was a scholar and a *littérateur*, and on the Bench he was at home. It is somewhat ironic, however, that during his twelve years' experience as a judge he should have been compelled to preside over many hundreds of criminal trials. It was said that he would have done better had he confined himself to civil causes. But Sir James Stephen took an exceptional interest in criminology, and he wrote a standard work on the criminal law.

The new judge began well, and quickly caused his presence to be felt. Criminals, especially those who specialised in wife-beating, were amazed and indignant at Stephen's severity. They protested that "Old Orkins" was quite enough to have up against them, and that Sir James' sentences were "crool." After all, they argued, Mr. Justice Hawkins was something of a character and a sportsman, and he had his redeeming features, such as fondness for the racecourse and for dogs. But this new judge, with the stern demeanour and the cold, hard voice, was a sort of professor who breathed the air of universities and who had apparently never condescended to mingle with the people on racecourses or anywhere else. Thus Mr. Justice Stephen was unpopular amongst the denizens of the dock, and when on circuit or at the Old Bailey the judge found that there was competition amongst the wrong-doers to get tried by another judge.

With " scenes " here and there and an occasional letter to the papers about his sentences, Mr. Justice Stephen jogged along until the year of jubilee. Then he came into contact with public opinion, and the first great battle was fought between him and his critics. Let us see what the battle was about and who won it.

In 1887 a hard-working Jewish couple, Isaac and Miriam Angel, lived in Batty Street, Whitechapel. They occupied a couple of rooms in a depressing tenement, and Isaac kept himself and his wife by means of his trade of boot-riveter. As they had two rooms in a district where a single one was regarded as a luxury it was popularly supposed that they were rich, and amongst those who believed this legend was Israel Lipski, who called himself a walking-stick maker, though he was described by candid friends as an inspector of pavements!

One June morning Mrs. Angel did not appear at her usual time, and as there is no solitude in an East End tenement her fellow-tenants became surprised at her absence. Surprise was soon replaced by anxiety, and at last one of her friends knocked on her door. There was no response; the handle was turned, and the door discovered to be locked on the inside.

This fact kindled the anxiety of Mrs. Angel's

friend. She was aware that the woman was expecting her first child, and she came to the conclusion that Mrs. Angel had been taken ill and was in an unconscious condition. Without hesitating another moment she burst the door in and ran to the bed, where she found Mrs. Angel lying on her back with her lips and her clothes stained, and showing no signs of life.

A doctor was summoned, and he could only pronounce life to be extinct, but he expressed the opinion that Mrs. Angel had been poisoned and that the wound on her head was not sufficient to have caused her death.

The sensations of the small group of excited women were weird. The mystery seemed profound. The door had been locked on the inside, and the murderer—if murder had been committed—could not have escaped by the window, because it was too high from the street.

But it was ridiculous to suppose that Mrs. Angel had first hit herself on the head and then had taken poison when the poison alone would have sufficed to end her life had she desired to commit suicide.

What could have happened ? Even the doctor was helpless in the face of the obvious facts, but quite unexpectedly the mystery was partially solved. The women had covered Mrs. Angel's face and were preparing to go, leaving the room in charge of the policeman who had just arrived, when suddenly they were startled out of their wits by a groan.

After the first feeling of astonishment a search was made by the policeman and the doctor, and from under the bed they dragged the unconscious form of a young man, whose lips and clothes were stained just like Mrs. Angel's. With all haste he was conveyed to the London

Hospital, and after a relapse which almost cost him his life he recovered, thanks to the skill of the medical staff.

It was obvious, of course, that Israel Lipski—he had written his name on a piece of paper at the hospital—was the one person who could throw any light on the mysterious death of Mrs. Angel, and he was immediately questioned about it.

He told a remarkable story. According to his version, two fellow-Jews had murdered Mrs. Angel and then had forced him to take a drink of spirits which had been mixed with a strong acid. When in a semi-unconscious condition he had been thrown under the bed, and the murderers had departed, their last words being, "Lipski will soon be dead, too."

The story was discredited at once. Lipski was a poor liar, for he forgot to take into consideration the fact that the door had been locked from the inside, and he could not have locked it himself whilst unconscious and returned to his position under the bed. He was, therefore, arrested, brought before the magistrates, and committed for trial.

Mr. Justice Stephen took his seat on the Bench at the Old Bailey, hardly expecting the case to last a day, but the defence was unexpectedly tenacious, and two days passed before a verdict was arrived at. It was proved that Mrs. Angel had been poisoned with impure nitric acid, that she must have suffered agonies before expiring, and that Lipski had purchased nitric acid from a chemist shortly before the murder. But the defence scored one point by the failure of the prosecution to prove that the actual bottle found on Mrs. Angel's bed had ever been in Lipski's hands.

The judge's summing-up gave those in court the impression that his opinion was that, whilst the gravest suspicion attached to the accused, the evidence against him was not sufficiently strong to warrant conviction, and when the jury retired the packed audience thought that they would have to wait hours for a decision—if a decision resulted. But the jury at any rate were not puzzled or doubtful, and in nine minutes they were back in court again, and their foreman was recording a verdict of guilty.

Within an hour of the passing of sentence of death the agitation in favour of a reprieve began. Extraordinary interest was suddenly taken in this illiterate Polish Jew, who had been proved to have murdered a woman for the sake of a few pounds.

The verdict of the jury was hotly contested. It was said that Lipski was innocent, and his supporters soon demanded release and not reprieve. They declared that Lipski had been convicted because he was a poor man and an alien, and all sorts of reasons and arguments were advanced to prove that a terrible miscarriage of justice would result if the convict were executed.

The most enthusiastic of the friends of Lipski was the late W. T. Stead. He was then editing the *Pall Mall Gazette*, and he filled columns day after day with attacks on the judge, jury, and the laws of the country. Daily the martyr's crown was conferred on the Polish Jew, and poor Mr. Justice Stephen was severely censured. Every weak point in the case for the Crown was mercilessly exposed and criticised, and all the time crowds of well-dressed persons were calling at the numerous offices where petitions for reprieve were lying and gladly attaching their signatures to them, so as to help to save an innocent man.

The agitation was cleverly stage-managed and extremely well worked up, but amid the turmoil Mr. Justice Stephen was quite unperturbed. He had verged too much on caution when addressing the jury at the trial, but after the verdict he made no secret of his concurrence with the opinion of the jury. Because of that he earned the animus of Mr. Stead, but it scarcely affected him.

Of course, the Home Secretary (then Mr. Matthews) had to investigate the circumstances —the public agitation for Lipski's release left him no option—but wisely he decided to consult the judge who had presided at the Old Bailey, A long consultation followed, and Stephen succeeded in convincing the Cabinet Minister that Lipski ought to suffer the extreme penalty of the law.

The announcement of the Home Secretary's decision was followed by a perfect howl from the Lipskians. They were more ferocious than ever, and they exhausted themselves with fury, but just when they were preparing a great demonstration in Hyde Park the astounding news arrived that Lipski had confessed !

The wretched convict's champions had no sooner recovered from their amazement than they began to express doubts. Lipski's confession, however, was published in full, and they instantly went in search of something more absorbing, and tried to forget how extremely foolish they had made themselves over a cowardly murderer.

The convict's confession is worth printing in full, in view of the fact that until it was actually written out some hundreds of thousands of respectable British citizens were proud to call themselves his champions.

On the Sunday after the governor of the prison had informed him of the Home Secretary's decision the convict wrote his account of the crime.

"I alone was guilty of the murder of Miriam Angel," he declared. "I thought she had money. The door was unlocked, and I entered. I had no thought of violating her. Miriam Angel awoke and cried out softly, so I struck her on the head and put my hand over her mouth. That morning I had bought a pennyworth of nitric acid to put an end to myself, and I remembered that it was in my pocket, so I took the bottle and poured most of it down the woman's throat. She fainted. I took the rest. Hearing people coming downstairs I locked the door on the inside and crawled under the bed. I fainted. Rosenbloom and Schmuss"—the two men he had accused in his original statement—"knew nothing of the crime." That was the document that scattered the legions of his champions and made most of them wish that they had never heard the name of Lipski.

Two years later Mr. Justice Stephen was again one of the principal figures in a controversy inspired by a great criminal trial. The result was not so satisfactory to him this time, and even to-day there are many who maintain that Mrs. Maybrick was perfectly innocent of the murder of her husband in 1889.

Mr. and Mrs. Maybrick were living in Battlecrease House, Liverpool, with their two children, and as they were well off and outwardly on good terms they were envied by their acquaintances, who did not know that Mrs. Maybrick had fallen in love with another man and that she and her husband were leading a "cat-and-dog life."

It is unnecessary to follow up the quarrels or dwell upon the fact that Mrs. Maybrick eloped with her lover to London and returned home within three days. The facts remain that, after a long period of family bickering, James Maybrick died in mysterious circumstances, and that the authorities considered they had sufficient evidence to justify the arrest of his widow.

With the arrest of the unhappy woman the "Maybrick case" became a public sensation, and the elopement with Brierly becoming known, everybody's hand was against the accused. She was hooted when the hideous police van took her to the police court, and with the shouts of execration of the indignant public in her ears she tottered into her lonely cell after the ending of each day's proceedings. If ever a woman was condemned before she was heard it was Florence Maybrick. Public opinion was dead against her, and it seemed that no power on earth could save her from conviction and execution.

St. George's Hall, Liverpool, was the scene of her final trial, and Mr. Justice Stephen presided. Sir Charles Russell, Q.C., afterwards Lord Chief Justice of England, and Mr. William Pickford, now Lord Sterndale and Master of the Rolls, defended the accused; whilst the prosecution was entrusted to Mr. Addison, Q.C., M.P., afterwards a County Court Judge.

For seven days a crowded court listened to a sordid story of intrigue, poison, and death. Specialists proved that arsenic had been found in the body of the deceased, and there were witnesses to relate how Mrs. Maybrick had bought fly-papers and had been seen extracting the arsenic from them.

Sir Charles Russell stood head and shoulders above the counsel engaged in the case, but, despite his searching cross-examination and brilliant winding-up speech, the accused was convicted and sentenced to death.

It might reasonably be supposed that the verdict of the jury would have been received with acclamation by the public, but as a matter of fact an extraordinary change in the public opinion occurred whilst Mrs. Maybrick was awaiting trial. She became a heroine, and her innocence was accepted as suddenly as her guilt had been decided upon in the first stages of the drama.

Anti-Maybrickites were in a small minority, and although during the trial popular opinion tended to sway backwards and forwards, the day that witnessed the conviction of the unfortunate woman found the believers in her innocence at their strongest. She had been hooted at the police court, but she was cheered outside St. George's Hall, where daily her followers assembled and called for acquittal.

For some reason, even now obscure, the Maybrickites decided that Mr. Justice Stephen was the principal cause of their discomfiture. It was true that in summing up he had made a few errors, but these had been instantly corrected by watchful counsel. However, Stephen, emerging from St. George's Hall to enter his carriage, was assailed by a mob, which attempted to carry him off, and only a strong force of police saved his lordship, who was badly shaken by the experience.

The agitation continued, and even when Mrs. Maybrick was reprieved it did not die down.

From time to time efforts were made to re-open the case, but without success, and it was not until she had served fifteen years' penal servitude that she was released. She is now in America.

The judge's enemies circulated a report that he was suffering from a mental illness which had stricken him down in 1885, and instantly "The Mad Judge," as some termed him ever afterwards, was the topic of many awesome stories. A mad judge trying a woman for her life! It made the credulous shiver.

Stephen ignored the newspaper attacks, and in the several discussions with the Home Secretary, who called him in to debate the question of reprieve or no reprieve, never condescended to refer to them. But he was not prejudiced against Mrs. Maybrick, and he advised Mr. Matthews to grant her a reprieve, and accordingly the hand of the executioner was stayed.

But for all his strength and pride the fierce agitation must have left its mark on him, for he was never the same man again. He did not slacken, and he was seldom absent from his post, but he began to show signs of feeling the strain, and now and again he would lose control of a case and forget what he was doing.

Once he sentenced a wife-beater to seven years' penal servitude, and the convict, an ignorant man, refused to leave the dock until he had pointed out to the judge that the sentence was, in view of the evidence, illegal. The judge instantly saw his error, and reduced the penalty to one of months. It was, perhaps, a trivial incident, but taken with many others was in reality most significant.

In 1891 he accompanied Lord Chief Justice

Coleridge on circuit, and the latter, who had read certain statements concerning the condition of his brother-judge, decided to draw his attention to them. It was a delicate task, but silver-tongued Coleridge was equal to it, and in the kindest manner possible he asked his friend and colleague if it would not be advisable to refute his slanderers by seeing a doctor and obtaining from him a statement that he was quite equal to his arduous duties.

Sir James was somewhat taken aback, but he immediately returned to London, and called on Sir Andrew Clark, the eminent doctor. His verdict was promptly given.

" You must retire from the Bench, Sir James," he said firmly, and the judge instantly sent in his resignation.

Those who knew him were very sorry for the sudden close of his career at an age—sixty-two—when many judges begin theirs, but Stephen did not complain, and the Government rewarding him with a baronetcy, he retired into private life. Three years later he died.

I have mentioned only his criminal trials, but a civil one which had far-reaching consequences must be mentioned.

In 1886 the Postmaster-General brought an action against the National Telephone Company claiming an injunction on the ground that the telephone was an infringement of his monopoly of the telegraph system. A number of great lawyers thereupon spent days arguing before Mr. Justice Stephen as to whether a telephone message was the same as a telegram. The company was, of course, fighting for its existence, for if the Postmaster-General gained the verdict it would mean an end of every telephone which was not the property of the State.

Thousands of pounds were spent by each side, and the judge had a difficult and complicated task.

The National Telephone Company was a great commercial concern, and it seemed that the action of the State was arbitrary and tyrannical, but Mr. Justice Stephen was not to be affected by such considerations. He was there to decide a point of law, and finally he gave judgment in favour of the State, and the National Telephone Company ceased to exist as an independent corporation.

The Postmaster-General, however, saved the situation by granting a long license to the company to work its telephones, and when this license expired the State took over the system, paying adequate compensation to the shareholders.

Sir James Stephen, therefore, may be said to have by a single decision—it was never contested in a higher court—nationalised the telephone, and, perhaps, if the Maybrick case is ever forgotten, he may be remembered for that.

CHAPTER IV

Sir Henry Hawkins

Because it fell to his lot to preside over many notable murder trials and to pronounce the sentence of death in all cases where the jury returned a verdict of guilty—it must be remembered that in this event the judge has no option as to the punishment to be meted out to capital offenders—Mr. Justice Hawkins was often described as " The Hanging Judge." But those who knew him were well aware that he was one of the kindest of men, and his popularity with the Bar and the Bench, not to mention the sporting fraternity, who liked him because he was fond of the turf, never waned.

In this connection I recall a scene at one of the Inns of Court in London some years ago, when about fifty students were waiting to be called to the Bar. The hall was filled that night with excited young men, a sprinkling of fully-fledged barristers and a few of the judges. All was animation, the crowd being divided up into numerous little groups discussing the events of the night. Suddenly the door at the far end of the hall opened, and the next moment a sturdy man of small stature entered with a curious shuffle. There was a moment's hush, and then a student jumped on a chair and began to sing. He had not finished the first line of the song when every student was bellowing at the top of his voice Albert Chevalier's famous song, "Mr. 'Enry 'Awkins is a first-class nime."

The little judge stood with a grim smile on his face, and waited patiently until the song had been finished. Then he turned to a brother judge and made a remark, and as they were laughing the signal was made that the serious business of the night was about to begin. The incident was over, but it was not without its significance, for it proved that Sir Henry Hawkins was one of the most popular men in his profession.

Sir Henry Hawkins—he became Lord Brampton in 1899—was born at Hitchin in 1817, and died in 1907 at the great age of ninety. His life covered a notable period, and that he was lucky as well as clever cannot be denied. Success came to him early, and he enjoyed it for over sixty years. Thirty-three years at the Bar were followed by twenty-two on the Bench, and after that he had nine more in the comfortable atmosphere of the House of Lords. It is a splendid record for the son of a country solicitor, and because it was due entirely to his own abilities Hawkins was justly proud of the great position to which he attained.

It is difficult to say exactly when Hawkins, the advocate, became really well known to the public, but his defence in the case of Dr. Simon Bernard, charged with having conspired with Orsini to assassinate Louis Napoleon, afterwards Napoleon III, drew more than ordinary attention to his supreme cleverness as a cross-examiner and an authority on the law. It also revealed his capabilities for fighting what appeared at first to be a hopeless case. Even his client, the fiery doctor, thought little of his chances, and was quite prepared to face his doom; but Hawkins girded himself for the fray, and, greatly to the surprise of the prisoner, snatched a verdict of acquittal from the jury.

Other difficult cases were brought to him. Many, of course, were merely fantastic attempts on the part of obviously guilty criminals to escape the consequences of their evil deeds, and Hawkins was helpless; but whenever there was a chance he made the most of it, and in the 'fifties and 'sixties of the last century no really big law case, criminal or civil, was considered complete without the presence of the brilliant barrister on one side or the other.

Socially, too, he was a success. Otherwise he would not have been invited to take part in the famous and now historic amateur theatricals which Charles Dickens staged at Knebworth, the country seat of Lord Lytton. Hawkins played only small parts, but had the felicity of making the acquaintance of some of the most prominent figures in Victorian society, and he never forgot his experiences as an actor in days which now seem so far away.

But his real business was the law, and even the charms of society could not lure him away from it. He had his way to make in the world, and as he had resolved to build up a fortune he worked day and night to achieve his purpose. And certainly he gave full value for his fees, big as they were, and before he was rich he was generous, with the generosity of the man who tries to do his best for a brother in distress.

Edwin James, the ill-fated barrister who met with disaster after becoming Q.C. and M.P., asked him to lend him fifteen hundred pounds. Emboldened by Hawkins' readiness, he coolly doubled his request, and although the younger man had to borrow the three thousand pounds he handed the money over, and, of course, never saw a penny of it again.

It was a heavy price to pay for having the doubtful honour of James' acquaintance. The two men had been associated in the defence of Sir J. D. Paul, the baronet banker, who got fourteen years for fraud, and on that occasion James, in the height of his reputation, was the leader and Hawkins only his junior. But their positions were reversed with a vengeance a few years later, when James, disbarred and bankrupt, was skulking about the law courts, and Hawkins, a judge of the High Court, was proving that he could be as brilliant on the Bench as he had been at the Bar.

But I do not intend to deal fully with Hawkins, the barrister. It is of the judge that I wish to write, though I will mention in passing that he defended Colonel Valentine Baker amongst others, and that his name will always be associated with the Tichborne case. Hawkins was retained in the latter to cross-examine the impostor, Arthur Orton, but at the last moment his junior, Coleridge, was appointed Solicitor-General, and by virtue of his office "led" Hawkins. The result was that Coleridge, not a brilliant cross-examiner, found himself outmatched by the cute butcher from Australia, and the lawsuit was protracted until it broke all records so far as time and money are concerned. However, when Arthur Orton had failed to obtain the Tichborne estates and was prosecuted for perjury, Hawkins was called in to conduct the prosecution for the Crown.

There was no mistake now, and the famous plaintiff received fourteen years' penal servitude. Shortly afterwards Hawkins was offered a judgeship, and declined it, but when two years later the offer was renewed he altered his mind, and on November 2nd, 1876, Henry Hawkins, Q.C., became Sir Henry Hawkins, judge of the High Court.

The first murder trial over which he presided was destined to earn undying notoriety in the annals of crime, a trial which reeked with the sensational and the sordid. All England was deeply interested in the trial of the two men and two women, who were charged with practically starving to death the semi-imbecile wife of one of them. Of course, I am referring to the "Penge mystery."

The story was an exceedingly painful one, and it profoundly moved the country. It appeared that Louis Staunton married Harriet Richardson for the only reason that she had a fortune of four thousand pounds. When he had secured this property he began to neglect his wife for a girl named Alice Rhodes, and subsequently, finding that Harriet clung rather more tenaciously to life than he desired —he wanted to marry Alice Rhodes—he conceived the hellish plot of taking his wife and children to an isolated house outside a Kentish village and there starving her to death. In the execution of this vile plot he was assisted by his brother Patrick and the latter's wife. It was owing to the merest chance that the crime was ever discovered. On the morning after Harriet's death a gentleman of the name of Casabianca was in the post office in Forbes Road, Penge, when a stranger entered to enquire where deaths had to be registered, adding unnecessarily that the deceased was a lady who had recently resided at Cudham. The mention of the latter name interested Mr. Casabianca at once because his wife's sister was supposed to be residing there and as he had heard she was badly treated by her husband it occurred to him that the lady whose death was to be registered might be Mrs. Louis Staunton, his wife's relative. He, accordingly, made enquiries, and his account of the relations between husband and wife led to the doctor refusing a certificate, and an inquest and a sensational trial were the direct results.

After the inquest Louis and his brother Patrick, the latter's wife, and Alice Rhodes, were arrested and committed to the Old Bailey to stand their trial.

It was only natural that little else should be discussed in Great Britain between the committal for trial and the proceedings at the Old Bailey. Lord Chief Justice Cockburn was so interested in it that he actually reserved the case for himself, but at the last moment the trial was postponed and when it was taken at the following sessions it fell to the lot of the junior judge on the Bench to preside.

The conduct of the case was in keeping with its importance. Sir John Holker, the Attorney-General, prosecuted on behalf of the State, and to assist him were Sir Hardinge Giffard (the late Lord Halsbury), and Mr. (now Sir Harry) Poland; while the four prisoners had the assistance of some of the ablest barristers of the day. Mr. Montague Williams and the late Sir Charles Matthews defended Louis Staunton, the husband of the murdered woman; Mr. (now Sir Edward) Clarke was for Patrick Staunton; and Mr. (afterwards Sir Douglas) Straight looked after the interests of Mrs. Patrick Staunton. Alice Rhodes, a sinister figure throughout the case, was ably defended by Mr. Gye.

As usual in great trials, some reputations were made. Mr. Justice Hawkins established his fame as a great judge, and Sir Edward Clarke convinced the world that he was an equally great advocate.

Curiously enough, only one man has impugned Hawkins' conduct of the trial of the Stauntons, and that man is Sir Edward Clarke. I heard him declare that Mr. Justice Hawkins was the worst judge before whom he had appeared, but in this opinion he stands alone. All the other famous barristers agree in saying that Sir Henry was one of the strongest, fairest, and most upright judges on the Bench.

It is unquestioned that he dominated the court throughout the long trial. He was the junior judge, but he might have been twenty years on the Bench by the way he handled the witnesses, the Bar, and all concerned. "There is a new force on the Bench," whispered the Attorney-General when Sir Henry began to sum up. When he had finished everybody in court was of one mind with Sir John Holker.

It was on Wednesday, September 26th, 1877, that the court assembled to hear the judge instruct the jury in his first murder trial, and at half-past ten he began in a clear, crisp tone. There was an interval for lunch, and another for tea, but it was not until twenty minutes to ten that night that he finished.

It was a masterly performance, and, if lengthy, did not contain a superfluous sentence. The evidence for and against was analysed in the fairest manner, and the jury retired with the knowledge that, difficult as the case was—the medical evidence on behalf of the prisoner undoubtedly puzzled them—the judge had solved many of its problems in his summing-up.

At ten minutes past eleven they returned and announced a verdict of guilty, and all four prisoners were sentenced to death in a hushed and excited court, crowded in every part and throbbing with excitement. Like many callous murderers, the convicts were terrified at the thought of death, and they collapsed in the dock. But they were destined not to be delivered to the hangman.

An agitation was started in their favour on the pretence that Harriet Staunton might have died of a brain affection. The medical profession supported the petition for reprieve—Charles Reade was one of the many who wrote fiery letters to the press—and eventually the woman Rhodes was pardoned, and the others sent to penal servitude for life.

Patrick Staunton died in prison, but his widow was released long before she had served the regulation fifteen years—the usual equivalent of a "life" sentence—and Louis Staunton survived his term, and was then let loose again on the world.

That the two men should have been executed goes without saying, for the evidence proved conclusively at the trial that they had persistently prevented Harriet Staunton eating enough to maintain life. They took full advantage of the poor creature's weak-mindedness to send her to a most horrible death.

The judge was blamed for having protracted the proceedings on the last day, and thereby harrowing the feelings of the prisoners by sentencing them to death amid the weird half-light of the old court. But he merely did his duty, and when the noise of partisans had died away it was universally acknowledged that in Mr. Justice Hawkins the country had a fearless and uncompromising upholder of its laws.

The "Penge mystery," by the way, did

incalculable harm to Penge. This was very bad luck, because, as a matter of fact, Harriet Staunton only lived there for a day. If it was necessary to identify the crime with a geographical name it ought to have been called the "Cudham mystery." But Penge secured the ghastly advertisement, and the result was that the place was avoided by hundreds who would in the ordinary course of events have become householders there and added to the prosperity of the South-East London suburb. Property depreciated, and slums came into existence. It was many years before Penge recovered from this unfortunate notoriety, and it is doubtful if it has shaken off the effects even now.

One of the most remarkable characteristics of the judge was his fondness for his famous dog, Jack. When on circuit Sir Henry was in the habit of getting up in the morning before six in order that he might take Jack for a long walk, and in many a provincial town the early workers often saw the sturdy figure of the judge walking briskly towards the open country with the dog by his side.

He loved the fresh air, except when occupied in his official duties. This was one of his peculiarities. The man who would walk five miles before breakfast because he would not trust any one else with his beloved dog would sit for a dozen hours in a stuffy little court packed to the doors and with every window shut tightly.

I once heard him angrily order an usher to close a window which was letting in the fresh air through a space not greater than a couple of inches. During the trials of the Stauntons and of Dr. Lamson it was the same. The little judge sat on the Bench and grimly surveyed a perspiring court, the only person at his ease in it. Every window was tightly shut, and he was happy.

Sir Henry Hawkins always knew his own mind. He did not "wobble." Therein lay his strength, and he had an astonishing gift for going straight to the point. And he appeared to be tireless. There was a case heard at Nottingham when he was nearly eighty, and, as usual, the stuffy little court was stuffier than usual owing to the judge objecting to the admission of fresh air. Hour after hour counsel talked, until they were exhausted. The jury showed signs of fatigue, and began to grumble. One of the counsel engaged thought he saw a way out of the difficult situation. Rising, and speaking in honeyed tones, he suggested that his lordship must be feeling the effects of the long sitting.

"We are perfectly willing and prepared to go on, my lord," he said, supporting himself by clutching at his desk, "but, in view of your lordship's advanced age, and——"

"Never mind about that," snapped Sir Henry, who knew, of course, that counsel and jury wished for an adjournment. "I feel quite all right. Proceed with your argument. I wish to finish the case to-night."

There was no help for it, and the hearing dragged on until after eleven.

Next morning Sir Henry left his lodgings at five with Jack at his heels and a gun over his shoulder, and he spent a couple of hours rabbit shooting.

As he was returning with a couple of rabbits suspended from his gun, two working men who had made the acquaintance of the judge in his court caught sight of him.

Transfixed by the sight of the gun and the rabbits, they remained petrified, until one exclaimed in the hearing of Sir Henry—

" Gorblime ! The old 'un's been poachin' ! "

One of Sir Henry Hawkins' most famous trials was that of Dr. Lamson, the poisoner, a clever, unscrupulous man, with considerable medical knowledge and a cunning and scheming brain. He had married a girl with a small fortune consisting of three thousand pounds. When he had squandered it and was quite penniless he remembered that his wife's brother, an invalid suffering from paralysis of the lower limbs, had three thousand pounds, and that if he died his sister—Mrs. Lamson—would inherit half of his fortune. Would young Percy John die before he came of age ? Lamson secretly resolved that he should, because he was desperately in need of money.

When a doctor takes to crime he finds himself less hampered than the ordinary criminal, and Lamson, backed by his medical degree, was able to purchase more than sufficient aconitine—a vegetable poison—to effect his purpose.

Percy John, his young brother-in-law, was still at school at Wimbledon, nineteen years of age, happy in his surroundings, and, despite his infirmity, a pleasant and cheerful companion. He was devoted to his sister and her husband, Lamson, and the latter's visits were always looked forward to with pleasure by the invalid, who never realised that the man he regarded as his dearest friend was planning his death.

At the time of the murder young John was going to spend the Christmas holidays with his sister and brother-in-law, and it wanted but a fortnight to the annual break-up when Lamson called unexpectedly at the school. He was in a genial humour, and chatted with all his usual charm, though greatly worried because he was heavily in debt. But he was young—only twenty-nine—and there was no reason why he should not, after all, become a successful practitioner.

The memorable visit which was to result in murder was marked by one or two peculiar incidents. To begin with, Lamson brought with him a Dundee cake, not as a present to his brother-in-law, but—so he said—in order to present him with a piece of it. When he took the cake out of the black bag it was seen to be already cut. This was odd, but he diverted attention by producing some capsules, which he said were good for the nerves, and he gave one to the headmaster of the school and another to Percy John, as well as taking one himself.

" Have a piece of cake," said Lamson to Percy, after the latter had swallowed the capsule, and, without waiting for an answer,cut a small piece of the cake with his penknife and handed it to the youth. This was astonishing enough, but it appears not to have aroused any suspicions. Yet a little reflection might have convinced the headmaster that a gentleman sitting in a parlour does not cut cake with a penknife which may have been used on a hundred and one different articles. And why did he not hand him the piece already cut ?

Of course, Lamson had secreted some of the deadly aconitine in a particular raisin in a certain part of the cake, and, having induced Percy to swallow a harmless capsule, followed it up by offering him a piece of poisoned cake. Only a medical man would have thought of concealing the poison in a raisin, the skin of which would resist digestion for some time and give the poisoner a good start.

Lamson wished to get away to Paris and wait there until the murdered boy was buried. He hoped that even if suspicion were directed against him the capsule he had given the boy to swallow would be searched for during the post-mortem, and its non-poisonous nature having been ascertained would clear his name. But he was too clever, and, fortunately for justice, his plans miscarried. Lamson left for Paris that night, but long before he arrived at his destination Percy John had died in great agony and the authorities were beginning to couple his brother-in-law's name with the crime. Lamson read an account in a London evening paper which he bought in Paris of what was termed "Mysterious Death of a Student at Wimbledon," and later he saw unpleasant prominence given to an interview with the headmaster in which his own name was mentioned more often than he liked. His position was perilous. He had no money and no friends. Capture would be certain and extradition would be only a matter of a few weeks at the utmost. He realised that he would have nothing to gain by avoiding the authorities, and, determining to try what bluff would do, he crossed the channel, drove to Scotland Yard, and somewhat surprised Chief Inspector Butcher by introducing himself as "Dr. Lamson whose name has been mentioned in connection with the death of Percy John."

An hour or so later the doctor, who had called in company with his wife, was placed under arrest, and the machinery of the law was set in motion. It finally brought him to the

Old Bailey, where he faced Mr. Justice Hawkins, and, after a fair trial and a brilliant defence by Montague Williams, he heard his doom pronounced by the judge.

A very remarkable feature of the case was the unselfish devotion of Lamson's young wife, the sister of the boy he had murdered. There is every reason to believe that she knew only too well that her husband was guilty, yet when all the world had turned against him she stood bravely by his side and used all the artifices of her sex and position to win a little sympathy for her husband. But all the sympathy she won was for herself. Everybody pitied and admired her, for they realised that she really loved the scoundrel in the dock, the father of her little baby girl.

It was hard to witness her agony during the six days of the trial. Towards the close Mr. Justice Hawkins conveyed a message indirectly to her that she ought to spare herself and retire, for by now there could be no possible doubt as to what the verdict of the twelve good men and true was to be. But she stuck to her post, and her hand-clasp and kiss to the bearded doctor in the dock gave each day's proceedings a touch of the pathetic which the case never lost, despite the terrible callousness of the prisoner.

Another doctor Hawkins tried and sentenced to death was Neill Cream, a very remarkable villain.

When Cream was residing in lodgings near Waterloo Station, there was living in the neighbourhood a girl named Matilda Clover, who may be described as being " no better than she ought to have been." Matilda in some mysterious way got to know Cream, and, ascertaining that he was a doctor, she asked him to treat her.

He promptly gave her a couple of pills containing sufficient strychnine to kill half a dozen people, and within a few hours of taking them the wretched girl died in fearful agony. This was on October 20th, 1891, and three days later the woman was buried, the certificate signed by her regular medical attendant ascribing her death to alcoholic poisoning.

Now Matilda had few friends or relations to mourn her, and when she passed there was no one to miss her, and the world would never have heard her name again had not a very distinguished doctor, no less a personage than Sir William Broadbent, M.D., received a letter signed "T. Malony," accusing him of having poisoned Matilda Clover. The writer of this queer communication was good enough to promise secrecy if Sir William would send him the sum of £2,500. Naturally enough, the doctor considered the letter to be the production of a lunatic. Nevertheless, he forwarded it to Scotland Yard, where it was placed amongst the archives. Public men are constantly the recipients of extraordinary letters, and the inspector into whose hands the "Malony" epistle fell attached even less importance to it than Sir William Broadbent had done.

Neill Cream was, of course, "T. Malony," but he did not follow up his letter to the doctor, for he was eager for more victims. Shortly after Matilda Clover's death another "mysterious affair" happened near Waterloo Station. A girl known as Ellen Donworth was conveyed to St. Thomas' Hospital in a dying condition, and before expiring she told how a strange gentleman had given her two pills. An inquest was held on Ellen's body, and arsenic and strychnine discovered, but the police had no clue, and it seemed that they would never get one, when a director of a well-known firm, who is to-day a member of the House of Lords, got a letter signed " W. Bayne," accusing him of having poisoned Ellen Donworth, but offering to destroy the proofs of his guilt for £300,000 !

The writer requested the gentleman to put a notice in the window of his premises in the Strand agreeing to his terms, but, although this was done, the detectives who haunted the building for many days and nights were never rewarded with a glimpse of " Mr. Bayne," who was really Neill Cream.

The latter had now committed two diabolical murders, and he thought that he deserved a holiday. So he took a trip to Canada, and previous to leaving he made a will in favour of a young lady with whom he had fallen in love. Later on, when the Malony and Bayne letters were suspected to be the work of the doctor, a comparison of their handwriting proved that they were the work of the man whose will was signed " Thomas Neill Cream."

Within four months the poisoner was back in London and looking for more victims, and when he became friendly with two young women, Alice Marsh and Emma Shrivell, he administered pills to them simultaneously. The following evening Cream spent hours reading the accounts of the double murder, and gloating over the helplessness of the police.

But Cream possessed a nervous, restless, and excitable disposition, and he was always anxious and haunted by fears. He was in a hurry to find some one he could accuse of being the murderer of the two women—the inquest on them was adjourned for a week—and he hit upon the plan of blackmailing the father of a young medical student who lodged in the same house as himself.

One morning the poisoner got into conversation with his landlady's daughter on the subject of murders. Gradually he introduced the name of his fellow lodger, and learnt that his father was a leading practitioner in Barnstaple. This was sufficient for Cream, and shortly afterwards he wrote a letter to the gentleman in Devonshire informing him that his son had poisoned Marsh and Shrivell, and that the writer had it in his power to destroy all the evidence and would do so for fifteen hundred pounds. It will be seen that he was merely repeating what he said to Sir William Broadbent and the wealthy business man, and the only variations were the amount demanded and the signature. In the case of the Devonshire doctor Cream signed himself "W. H. Murray."

The extraordinary and silly letter was on its way to Barnstaple when Neill Cream met an acquaintance who was an engineer, and at once referred to the murders, which were exciting public interest.

"I know the guilty man," said Cream confidently. "Ay, and I know also that he poisoned another woman, Loo Harvey."

"Indeed!" exclaimed his friend in astonishment. "Then why don't you go to Scotland Yard and see an inspector about it."

"Because I don't wish to be mixed up in such a horrible business," was the prim reply. "But if you'll come with me I'll show you the house where Loo Harvey used to live."

On the way Neill Cream positively stated that his fellow lodger was the criminal for whom the police were searching, and he named him to the astonished engineer. When they arrived outside the house where Loo Harvey had resided Cream became dramatic.

"That was the home of the poor girl," he said excitedly, "and the father of her murderer, a well-known doctor, is trying to save his son from exposure and arrest."

There was something so queer about his informant's manner that the engineer hesitated to take him seriously, but when Cream insisted upon giving him fuller details and named the music hall where Loo Harvey had met the doctor's son by appointment, the astonished listener considered it his duty to report the matter to the police.

At Scotland Yard he was received by Detective-Sergeant M'Intyre, a clever Scotsman, who had helped to solve many puzzling cases, and to him he recounted what his friend had told him, suppressing, however, Cream's name, as he had promised him he would.

"That's strange," said the detective thoughtfully. "No person of the name of Loo Harvey has been reported to us as having died under suspicious circumstances. You must have made a mistake. However, your statement will be filed in case anything turns up, and I will dispatch an officer to make enquiries for this Loo Harvey."

He carried out his promise, and a shrewd officer was ordered to proceed to the house which Loo Harvey was said to have lived in, but when he got there he could obtain no information, and the enquiry dragged on for two months without producing any results.

Meanwhile the Barnstaple doctor read the letter signed by "W. H. Murray" and wondered why a lunatic should bother him. He communicated with his son, and both of them agreed to take Scotland Yard into their confidence.

Accordingly " W. H. Murray's " letters—he wrote more than one—were delivered at the headquarters of the police, and, by a coincidence, Detective-Sergeant M'Intyre was given charge of them. Now the latter already had a letter of Murray's, for one had been addressed to the coroner of the jury who had investigated the deaths of Marsh and Shrivell, stating that the medical student was the murderer of the unfortunate girls.

But the police had as yet no real clue as to the identity of the murderer. Not a single one of them had ever heard of Neill Cream, and they were not looking for any one who resembled him, but when most puzzled they were destined to have a piece of luck which was to make clear all that was dark before and lead them to complete success.

M'Intyre was in his office when a constable announced that a gentleman wished to see him to make a complaint. The gentleman was Neill Cream, and he had a long story to tell of persecution.

" People are following me about," he said in a nervous tone, and watching the detective slily. " Morning, noon and night they worry me. When I look out of my bedroom window before dressing I see them, and late at night they are still there. Can't you do something to spare me this annoyance ? "

A Scotland Yard man has to be all things to all men, and M'Intyre soothingly promised his aid.

" You'd better leave me your name and address," he said quietly, " and later I'll come and see you."

"My name is Thomas Neill Cream," said the caller, who had difficulty in controlling himself, "and I am a commercial traveller."

"Very good," remarked the detective, holding out his hand. "Good-bye, Mr. Cream. I will personally look into this affair, and I think I will be able to protect you from the men who are worrying you."

Now, many persons call at Scotland Yard on similar errands to that which took Cream there, but there was something that stamped the latter as being quite different from the ordinary individual with a grievance, and M'Intyre, with true detective instinct, decided to delve into the history and habits of the "commercial traveller." He therefore asked certain of his colleagues if they knew anything about Neill Cream, and he felt rewarded when he was informed that the constable who had been on duty in the street where Marsh and Shrivell had resided at the time of their murder, had expressed the opinion that Cream was rather like the man he had seen leave the fatal house in the early hours of the morning.

"Hello, Mr. Cream, how are you?" Detective-Sergeant M'Intyre shook hands cordially with the somewhat mystified man, who took several seconds to recall his features. But when he did he smiled from sheer relief.

"I'm quite well, thank you," he said, becoming animated.

"Have you been bothered lately by those chaps?" was the detective's next question, delivered with a careless good humour that completely took the other off his guard.

"No, they must have been scared away by you," said Cream briskly. "It's a relief to be able to walk the streets of London without having men dogging one's footsteps. My nerves were beginning to——"

"Step in and have a drink with me," said M'Intyre, and the doctor, who loved a chat, willingly accepted the invitation.

In the bar parlour M'Intyre found two friends. One was an inspector and the other a constable —the latter the man who had seen the murderer of Marsh and Shrivell depart from the scene of his crime. Of course they were there by arrangement, but the detective pretended it was a chance meeting, and very soon the quartette were talking like old acquaintances. Cream was too much of a gossip to notice that he seldom let the others get a word in, but he contradicted himself so often that eventually the question arose as to whether he was a commercial traveller or not.

"I'll prove it by fetching my samples from my lodgings," exclaimed the doctor, rising to his feet.

When he had gone the three officers discussed the advisability of taking him into custody, but M'Intyre pointed out that the evidence against him in their possession was very weak.

"We'll give him a little more scope," he said finally. "He's been complaining to me of being shadowed, but he'll never stir a foot in future without a detective seeing him."

Forty-eight hours later M'Intyre received from the Devonshire doctor the letter signed "W. H. Murray," and he saw that the handwriting was the same as that of the letters which had been addressed to Sir William Broadbent.

"If Cream wrote them I'll serve a warrant against him," said the detective, and to his surprise discovered that the writing did not resemble the suspect's at all. This was a check, but M'Intyre was not dismayed. He noticed that the paper was of special quality and design, and he spent days trying to trace the manufacturer of it. His enquiries led him to cable to the police at Quebec, who answered that the water-mark was that of a mill in Canada which did not export any of its products to Europe, and that only some one who had been in Canada recently could be in possession of samples of it.

This was getting hot with a vengeance, but the detective wished to make sure, and one morning he visited Cream in his lodgings to have a chat with him, apologising for taking the doctor unawares and before he had risen for the day.

"By the way, old chap," he said with a laugh, "you might scribble a few lines for me."

The doctor did so, and M'Intyre, holding the paper up to the light, saw that the water-mark was the same as that of the letters signed "W. H. Murray." He was satisfied that he was on the right track now.

The poisoner, secretly perturbed by the detective's presence and yet desirous of appearing quite unconcerned, invited him to remain while he had breakfast, and when the meal was over and the conversation flagged, the murderer, as if unable to control his tongue, suddenly blurted out: "I'm going for a few days' holiday in the country—do you think I will be arrested before I go?"

"Why do you ask me that?" exclaimed M'Intyre with an amused smile. "Why should you be arrested?"

"I don't know," answered the doctor, doubtless wishing that he had bitten his tongue off before making such a dangerous remark. "But

I have an idea that I am being shadowed again, and it's very upsetting."

"If you'll be guided by me," said the officer pleasantly, "you'll come along to Scotland Yard and inquire there if there's anything against you."

"That seems sensible advice," Cream observed, deceived by his manner. "I'll go if you'll come along with me."

M'Intyre expressed his willingness to oblige him, and the two men set out together, but when they were nearly at Whitehall Cream stopped.

"I won't go any further," he said doggedly. "I don't believe that you are straight with me."

"Oh, very well," said the detective indifferently, "if you think that, we had better part."

With a sigh of relief the poisoner retraced his steps and M'Intyre went on to the Yard, but the doctor failed to observe that there was a tall, rather good-looking young man following him, and that on the other side of the road was another who was prepared to relieve his colleague should the latter be spotted by his quarry.

The authorities at Scotland Yard had by now grasped the full importance of the Neill Cream affair, for an inspector had recollected the letters addressed to Sir William Broadbent and the other gentleman, and the result was that Matilda Clover's body and Ellen Donworth's had been exhumed, and poison had been found in them. They were likewise convinced that the poisoner was Thomas Neill Cream, doctor of medicine, who called himself a commercial traveller in order to prevent the suspicion arising that he had the power to become possessed of deadly poisons.

Three days after the brief and dramatic colloquy with Detective-Sergeant M'Intyre the doctor decided that he would put the Atlantic between himself and Scotland Yard, but just as he was finishing his packing two detectives entered the room and informed him that they had a warrant for his arrest, and that the charge was sending a blackmailing letter to a certain doctor practising at Barnstaple.

"Blackmail!" exclaimed the prisoner, in astonishment, and the momentary terror faded from his face. He had expected something different, but when he appeared before the Bow Street magistrate for the second time he knew the worst, for the charge had been altered to wilful murder, and the names of his four victims were read out in open court.

The arrest caused an immense sensation, and whenever Neill Cream was brought up at Bow Street the court was packed. The story was told by the prosecution of the deliberate methods of the poisoner, and his amazing letters to Sir William Broadbent and other notabilities staggered the public, who had never heard the like before; but the weirdest surprise took place at the fourth hearing when counsel declared that there was strong suspicion against the accused of having murdered a fifth woman of the name of Loo Harvey. Instantly there came a movement at the back of the court, and a girl in the early twenties rose to her feet.

"I am Loo Harvey," she exclaimed, and everybody stared at her as though she had come back from the dead.

She gave a remarkable account at Bow Street and at the Old Bailey of her relations with Neill Cream. He had described himself to her as a doctor, and had handed her two pills to take as they stood on Waterloo Bridge. Something, however, caused her to feel suspicious of his motive, and although he insisted upon seeing her swallow them she managed to make a show of following his instructions whilst actually throwing them away from her. Then they had parted, the doctor feeling sure that she would die, and the girl to leave her lodgings, and, under another name, to live in a distant part of the city.

The trial began at the Old Bailey on October 17th, 1892, before Mr. Justice Hawkins, and of the four prosecuting counsel one only survives in the person of Lord Coleridge, now a judge of the High Court. Sir Henry Sutton, Sir C. F. Gill, K.C., and Sir Charles Russell, then Attorney-General, were the others.

It was in all respects a sensational and absorbingly interesting drama, although the meanest figure of all was the prisoner in the dock. Had Neill Cream lived thirty years later he would have been deemed insane, but he was regarded in the early nineties as a monster who had to be exterminated.

The case against him was proved fully, and the way Detective-Sergeant M'Intyre marshalled his facts did him great credit. Thanks mainly to his perseverance and industry, the Crown were able to trace the chemists' shops in Canada where the accused had obtained his poisons, while his authorship of the various letters was established, particularly those which were not in his handwriting. M'Intyre had solved the mystery surrounding the origin of "W. H. Murray's" epistles, for he had guessed that Cream had persuaded some woman who was infatuated with him to write them at his dictation, and what was more natural than that the girl to whom he was engaged and in whose favour he had made his will should be his secretary!

This young lady informed the court that Cream had persuaded her to write and sign the letters "W. H. Murray" and had given her a very plausible explanation of his motive for making such an odd request of her. Of course she was not blamed by any one, for, if she had erred, she was more than sufficiently punished by being brought into such a case, and the story of her wooing by a murderer published far and wide.

Mr. Justice Hawkins in his summing up briefly disposed of the long and ingenious speech Cream's leading counsel had made in his favour, and his lordship plainly told the jury that they ought to convict. It is very doubtful, however, if they needed any direction, for the facts were plain, and it took them merely ten minutes to agree formally to a verdict of guilty.

The Muswell Hill murder case also came before Hawkins, but it is unnecessary to do more than outline briefly the story of a remarkable criminal trial.

Milsom and Fowler, two desperate and scoundrelly ruffians, broke into the house of an old man named Smith. When the latter attempted to defend his property he was brutally murdered. The trial itself was remarkable for the assault Fowler made on his fellow-prisoner in the dock. It appeared that Fowler had got the impression that Milsom was anxious to turn Queen's evidence, but, as a matter of fact, the authorities had no intention of allowing either man to escape. Half way through the proceedings Fowler, snarling like a wild beast, hurled himself upon Milsom and clutched him by the throat. He was shaking the life out of the terrified wretch when half a dozen warders came to Milsom's assistance, and after a tremendous struggle parted the two men. It was indeed about the most amazing scene ever witnessed in the Old Bailey dock. The two men were, of course, executed after conviction. The ruffians suffered along with a third murderer—Seaman—and the prison authorities, apprehensive of another attempt by Fowler to assault Milsom, placed Seaman on the scaffold between the two former companions in crime.

"First time I've ever acted as a peace-maker," Seaman was heard to mutter as the bolt was drawn.

Sir Henry's "interesting cases" are so numerous that it is difficult to pick and choose, but in his last year on the Bench—1898—he tried Walter Horsford, the St. Neots murderer, as callous a ruffian as the history of crime can show.

It was an instance of a man finding his love for a woman growing cold, and when he had married another resolving to take the life of his first love.

Horsford had promised to marry Annie Holmes, a widow of thirty-eight, who was having a hard time with poverty. She fondly hoped that Horsford, a prosperous farmer, would marry her and provide for herself and her children. He said he would, and, although he managed to postpone the question of actual marriage, Mrs. Holmes never forgot to remind him that she expected him to make "an honest woman of her" one day.

But, as I have said, Horsford married some one else, and because he did not want his wife to know of his relations with Annie Holmes, he poisoned her with strychnine. Of course, no one saw him administer the poison—that was impossible—but after the woman's death a packet containing strychnine was found, on the cover of which were directions as to taking in the handwriting of the deceased. Other evidence further implicated Horsford, and he was arrested.

The defence laboured to show that the circumstantial evidence was weak, but Mr. Justice Hawkins very properly pointed out that in his extensive experience of murder trials he had never yet known a case where the actual murder had been witnessed by a third party, and that if it were necessary that to prove a crime an eye-witness of it must be produced in court ninety per cent. of murderers would escape.

There was no doubt of the judge's attitude in this particular case, and charges of unfairness were hurled against him, but he maintained his point, and the jury agreed with him, for Horsford was convicted and sentenced to death. When the convict confessed his guilt the last was heard of criticisms of the judge's policy.

After twenty-two years on the Bench Sir Henry Hawkins retired in 1898. He was now eighty-one, but in full possession of his faculties and remarkably vigorous for his age, and when in 1899 the late Queen Victoria conferred a peerage on him he welcomed the honour because it enabled him to take part in the deliberations of the highest court of all—the House of Lords.

In connection with the conferment of a peerage an amusing story is told. There was a more or less informal gathering of relations at the ex-judge's house to discuss the important question as to what title he should assume. His own inclination was to keep his name—the name which he had made famous—and he would have done so had not a friend remarked—

"Call yourself Lord 'Awkins of 'Itchin, 'Erts? Why, there's not a Cockney who'll be able to pronounce your new name correctly."

That settled it, and the title of Lord Brampton was chosen, and in his new disguise he lived until 1907. But no one ever thought of him as Lord Brampton. The name of Hawkins was too well known for that, and it was generally used in the newspapers, with the title in brackets. It seemed as though the great British public agreed with Mr. Chevalier that "Mr. 'Enry 'Awkins was a fust-class nime," and the old judge did not disagree with them.

CHAPTER V

LORD PRESIDENT INGLIS

JOHN INGLIS, the greatest of Scottish judges, was born in George Square, Edinburgh, on 21st August, 1810. Dr. Inglis, his father, was one of the ministers of Old Greyfriars parish, and he gave all his children a first-class education, but John was the clever boy of the family, and after Edinburgh High School—that nursery of Scottish judges—and Glasgow University he entered Baliol College, Oxford, where he subsequently took his M.A. and D.C.L. degrees. He was, therefore, well endowed with scholarship and brains when in 1835 he was called to the Bar, and, gifted, brilliant, and popular as he was, there was never any real doubt about his future.

The tall, slender figure of the young barrister, his sallow features, and his bright, compelling glance, added to his personal qualities, soon made him a conspicuous figure in the crowd of contestants for the positions which older men were surrendering either through promotion or death.

John Inglis could speak eloquently, but to the point; he had a persuasive manner and a charming personality. Nothing perturbed him. He was born to wear the wig and gown and sway a court, and it is not to be wondered at that he should have speedily attained to a comfortable practice.

When we remember that for at least fifty out of the eighty-one years of his life Inglis was a well-known public man, it will be realised how difficult it is to give an adequate idea of his pre-eminence. Long before the general public knew his name his rising to address the court was a signal for that court to fill.

"Young Inglis is talking," would be whispered, and even old men who had long since gained all the honours they wished for would be eager to hear him. This would have spoiled most men, but success only brought out the best in John Inglis.

The first law case of national importance in which Inglis was engaged was the trial of Alexander Humphreys for forgery.

Humphreys, the son of an English merchant, was an ex-schoolmaster who suddenly descended upon Scotland one day and claimed to be the Earl of Stirling, an ancient title which had lain dormant for many years. For a time he was left in possession of the earldom, but the then Earl of Rosebery, becoming jealous for the prestige of the peerage, moved in the House of Lords for a committee to inquire into the claims of the so-called "Earl of Stirling."

The law officers of the Crown thereupon brought an action against Humphreys and his agent. This was tried before Lord Cockburn, who gave judgment against the claimant. Declining to recognise that he was beaten, the "Earl" renewed his claim, and this time he produced the necessary documentary proofs which had been missing at the first trial. But these were discovered to be forgeries, and Alexander Humphreys was accordingly placed in the dock at Edinburgh and made to answer to the charge of forging and fabricating certain documents. The case lasted five days, and John Inglis was one of the three counsel engaged on the prisoner's behalf. As usual in these affairs, public sympathy was with Humphreys, and the result of the case was that whilst the jury found the papers to have been forged, they acquitted the prisoner of any knowledge of their real origin, and he was set free. On hearing the verdict he fainted in the dock.

Although only junior counsel, Inglis was able to make his presence felt in this *cause célèbre.* It would, indeed, have been difficult for a person with his compelling personality to hide his light under a bushel, and the Stirling trial added to his fame, reputation, and the number of his briefs.

One of his greatest legal triumphs gave to Scotland the honour of revolutionising the iron trade and at the same time increasing enormously the profits of the Scottish ironmasters.

The trial is known as " The Hot Blast Case," and it was a fight between the Neilsons, the Glasgow firm, and the Bairds, the great English ironmasters. The latter claimed to have the exclusive right to a certain invention which was of vital importance in the manufacture of iron, but the Glasgow firm had positive proof that for years they had used this particular process and were in fact the first people to adapt it to their requirements. However, Bairds had the patent, and they were determined to prevent the Scottish firm continuing to use the process, and accordingly they brought an action in Edinburgh.

Inglis was retained on behalf of the Neilsons, and he fought for his clients with all the resources of his well-equipped brain and splendid eloquence. He maintained that prior use invalidated the claims of the Bairds. No one disputed the fact that the Neilsons had been the first users, and Inglis had, therefore, not a difficult task.

It was naturally assumed that he would gain the verdict, but to his astonishment it was given in favour of the Bairds. The mistake was in reality caused by a misdirection of the Lord Justice-Clerk (Hope), a judge for whom Inglis had never had any regard.

Hope was a man of small talents and great connections, and it was the influence of the latter which had accelerated his amazing progress at the Bar. That a barrister with an unimportant practice should have been Solicitor-General for Scotland at the age of twenty-nine speaks volumes for the affection John Hope inspired in his many noble and legal relatives.

But it was not to be expected that Inglis, bristling with talent, should have tolerated a man greatly inferior to himself. Not that he displayed his feelings openly. From his youth to his venerable old age Inglis was ever the very perfection of politeness. The humblest and the highest met with the same gentle, courteous treatment at his hands, and only once did he display any temper in his relations with the Bench.

Hope was the judge in question, and he offended Inglis so much that the advocate—it was not, of course, during the Hot Blast Case—flung down his brief and declared that never again would he appear in any court presided over by the Lord Justice-Clerk. Only a private letter of explanation and apology from Hope caused Inglis to cancel his threat. We may be sure that the provocation must have been very severe for Inglis to have adopted this course. No public man ever bore affronts with greater patience; indeed, when now and then envy did speak of the great advocate and judge, all it could say against him was that at times he had been too meek.

An appeal by Neilsons succeeded, and Inglis' contention was upheld. Henceforth they were able to continue and expand their trade unhampered by any interference from their English rivals. It was a notable victory, and the effects were felt for years.

But, however important a civil cause may be, it is the criminal work that attracts public attention and leads to advancement. This has been denied, but one has only to take the names of a dozen famous lawyers and judges, and see how they achieved success.

It is said that Inglis' first appearance for the defence in a criminal charge was at Perth in 1836, when a railway engine-driver was charged with culpable homicide. A friend of the driver had asked his permission to be allowed to ride on his tender, and as a result of the driver's good nature in giving way the inexperienced friend lost his life.

Inglis made short work of the prosecution in an incisive speech, and the charge was abandoned and the prisoner "restored to his family."

A more important case was that of Dr. Wielobycki, an Edinburgh practitioner, who appears to have imagined that any death-bed patient he attended ought to leave him a legacy. The doctor, despite his foreign origin, had a large practice in Edinburgh, but not satisfied with his legitimate gains he began to forge wills in the names of dead patients. As each will bequeathed him a handsome legacy suspicions were aroused, and eventually the enterprising medico found himself in the dock.

Inglis was retained at once to make the best of a hopeless case, and his conduct of the defence, his masterly cross-examination, and his brilliant speech stamped him at once as a great criminal lawyer. All that human skill and eloquence could do were done on behalf of the prisoner, but facts were too strong, and Wielobycki was given fourteen years.

He was more successful in his defence of Dr. Smith, of St. Fergus, who was charged with the murder of a friend and patient whose life he had insured. It was a case full of difficulties and complications, and it is safe to say that no other advocate of the day could have secured the doctor's acquittal.

Meanwhile, Inglis was advancing in political reputation. In 1852 he was Solicitor-General, and contested Orkney and Shetland as a Conservative. He was, however, beaten, and that year found him Lord Advocate and—when his party went out of office—Dean of Faculty. One of his electioneering speeches contained a brief reference to his own career, and it is worth producing :

"I embarked in the legal profession without family influence or hereditary wealth. I embarked on my own resources, and, thank God I have succeeded hitherto. But even on such an occasion as this I must not forget that my father left me a legacy which I have ever held to be a jewel of great price. He left me his name—a name which he had taught the world to respect as that of a thoroughly honest and honourable man, and I may truly say that it has been the great object of my life to maintain the name pure and unsullied as I received it."

In the year 1857 John Inglis was Dean of Faculty, and at the height of his fame as an advocate. He did not frequent Edinburgh society, but that did not lessen his popularity with all classes. He had the remarkable gift of being able to adorn any office, however great.

Inglis could rise to the occasion, no matter how important the occasion was, and he had none of the desk-thumping, screaming methods which were so popular fifty years ago. Sometimes opposing counsel would enter court in a bad temper, determined to upset Inglis if they could. Within an hour they would have fallen under the spell of the Dean of Faculty, and had they been asked to explain how it had happened they would have been unable to do so. There was no resisting Inglis, because he was always just himself.

His reputation as the first criminal lawyer of the day was so well established that from the moment Madeleine Smith was arrested on the charge of having poisoned her lover, Emile L'Angelier, her family realised that there was only one advocate equal to the task of leading her defence. They resolved to secure the Dean of Faculty, and had Mr. Smith not been a rich man he could not have retained Inglis, who at this time was overwhelmed with the most remunerative business. He had the pick of the best briefs, and his consulting practice was an enormous one.

It is doubtful if he was anxious for criminal work, but he succumbed to the pleadings of the Smith family, and inspired by an innate chivalry threw himself into the cause of the prisoner with a zest which would have been remarkable in a much younger man.

Inglis had defended scores of prisoners during his twenty-two years as an advocate, but it was not until Madeline Smith became his client in 1857, that he held a consultation within the precincts of a prison. To satisfy himself as to her character he had an interview with her, and they chatted amiably about the defence and even general topics, and when he came away was firmly convinced that she was incapable of the terrible crime with which she was charged. Madeleine Smith was a remarkable person, but her greatest feat was her conversion of Inglis to a belief in her absolute innocence.

The public were, of course, on the side of the accused. She was a pretty Scottish girl of good education and position, and the man she was supposed to have poisoned was an adventurer of French origin, but public sympathy alone would not suffice to save her from conviction, and Inglis did not leave anything to chance when he studied his brief. Next to her advocate's speech, the feature of the trial was the reading of her letters to her lover, letters which for passion and self-revelation are without parallel. They would fill a book, but a few may be quoted to show her infatuation for the man she poisoned when he proved inconvenient and unnecessary.

"Glasgow, December 3rd, 1855.

"My own darling husband,—I am afraid I may be too late to write to you this evening, so as all are out I shall do it now, my sweet one. I did not expect the pleasure of seeing you last evening, of being fondled by you, dear, dear Emile. Our cook was ill, and went to bed at ten—that was the reason I could see you—but I trust ere long to have a long, long interview with you, sweet one of my soul, my love, my all, my own best beloved. I hope you slept well last evening, and find yourself better to-day. was at St. Vincent Street to-day. B. and M.

are gone to call for the Houldsworths and some others. Never fear me, I love you well, my own sweet darling Emile. Do go to Edinburgh and visit the Lanes—also, my sweet love, go to the ball given to the officers. I think you should consult Dr. M'Farlan—that is, go and see him, get him to sound you, tell him what is wrong with you. Ask him to prescribe for you—and if you have any love for your Mimi, follow his advice, and oh! sweet love, do not try and doctor yourself—but oh! sweet love, follow the M.D.'s advice—be good for once, and I am sure you will be well. Is it not horrid cold weather? I did, my love, so pity you standing in the cold last night, but I could not get Janet to sleep—little stupid thing. This is a horrid scrawl, as I have been stopped twice by that bore—visitor. My own sweet beloved, I can say nothing as to our marriage, as it is not certain when they may go from home, or when I may go to Edinburgh, it is uncertain. My beloved, will we require to be married (if it is in Edinburgh) in Edinburgh or will it do here? You know I know nothing of these things. I fear the banns in Glasgow, there are so many people know me. If I had any other name but Madeleine it might pass—but it is not a very common one. But we must manage in some way to be united ere we leave town. How kind of Mary to take any trouble with us. She must be a dear, good creature. I would so like to visit her, but no, I cannot. I shall never forget the first visit I paid my own beloved husband, my own sweet, dear Emile—you sweet, dear darling. If ever again I show temper (which I hope to God I won't) don't mind it—it is not with you I am cross. Sweet love, I adore you with my heart and soul. I must have a letter from you soon.

I am engaged up till Friday night. Sweet pet, will that be too soon for you to write ? I have written a great many letters to-day. I am much behind in my correspondence. I do hope your finger is better, take care of it. When may we meet again ?—soon, soon, I hope and trust. Sweet darling, you are kind to me, very kind and loving. I ought never in any way to vex or annoy you. My own, my beloved Emile, I wish to get this posted to-night, as I don't understand the post. I posted your Saturday note before twelve, and you did not get it till Monday. We have had a great many letters going astray lately. I got a letter on Monday morning written six weeks ago. Are these officers nice fellows ? Why are they here ? How is your mother and sister ?—well, I hope, my own sweet. But, pet, I must stop, as they will be in shortly. If I do not post this to-night you shall have a P.S. Much, much love, kisses tender, long embraces, kisses, love. I am, thy own ever fond, thy own dear, loving wife, thy

" MIMI L'ANGELIER."

" Glasgow, Tuesday, 29th April, 1856.

" My own, my beloved Emile—I wrote you Sunday night for you to get my note on your birthday (to-day), but I could not get it posted. Disappointment it was to me—but ' better late than never.' My beloved, may you have very, very many happy returns of the day—and each year may you find yourself happier and better than the last, and may each year find you more prosperous than the last. I trust, darling, that on your next birthday I may be with you to wish you many happy returns in person. May you, dearest, have long life. My constant prayer shall be for your welfare and continued good health. I hope you continue to feel better. My cough is a little better, sometimes quite away, but on the cold days it comes back. On Sunday I was at church, and in the afternoon Jack and I had a walk for four miles. Now, when I can walk four with a brother I could walk eight with my own beloved husband and not be fatigued. Yes, darling, we shall take very long walks. P. is not at all well, and very cross, and he won't go to bed and get better. So I tell him he deserves to be ill. To-morrow Houldsworth senior is to be with us, and some more old gentlemen I don't know, and a good many of the Row people to dinner, and on Monday we are to have a host of friends from Perthshire. I cannot tell you how tired I am of friends. I wish we were more alone. I wish I were with you alone, that would be true happiness. Dearest, I must see you, it is fearful never to see you—but I am sure I don't know when I shall see you. We shall spend an hour of bliss. There shall be no risk, only C. H. shall know. Friday is a holiday, so James and Janet are to come down on Thursday. Poor Jack cannot get away now. Do you know the office he had gone to—M'Celland, Ingram Street? Have you heard of de M. since his marriage? I see by the papers he was not married in church. Why not? I don't like marriages in the house. I have never seen a marriage in Scotland. I have been to many in London. Dearest, how I picture our marriage day. Where would you like to go the day we are married? I don't fancy a place in particular, so you can fix that when the time comes. I hope it may yet turn out September. I asked P. if I were to be married, if the banns would be in Row Church. And he said, No, I had nothing to do with the Row parish, I did not belong to it. So, darling, it would not require to be here—it could never be here—it would not do. I don't in the least mind if they won't give their consent, for I know very well they shall be the first to give in. I have got my *Chambers' Journal* for this month, and the article you mentioned is not in the April number, so it shall be in the May volume. I have been reading *Blackwood* for this month. B. is a favourite publication of mine ; in fact I think it is the best-conducted monthly publication. I have only got the length of Henry VIII in 'Hume,' and I agree with you it would not make a careless person become good. But it is a well-written history. Have you read Macaulay's third and fourth volumes ? I like the fourth very much. I am rather fond of comparing different authors on the same subject, so I am at present comparing 'Alison,' 'Hume,' and 'Macaulay.' Only fancy, in turning out an old box yesterday, I found an old notebook three years old, and in going over it, many of the pages had the name of L'Angelier on them. Now, that is long before I knew you. I did not think I had been so fond of my darling then. I put it in the fire, as there are so many names in it I would not like to see beside your own, my sweet darling husband. Now, this is a very long letter to-night. I must conclude with a fond, fond embrace, a dear, sweet kiss. I wish it were to be given, not sent. Kindest, warmest love to you, my husband dear. A kiss ! Another ! Oh to be in thy embrace, my sweet Emile ! Love again to thee from thy very fond, thy loving and ever devoted Mimi, thine own wife."

"May 3rd, 1856.

"My own, my beloved Emile,—The thought of seeing you so soon makes me feel happy and glad. Oh! to hear you again speak to me—call me your wife—and tell me you love me. Can you wonder that I feel happy. I shall be so happy to see you. I cannot tell how I long to see you—it looks such an age since I saw you, my own sweet pet. I am well. Cold quite gone. P. has been in bed two days. If he should not feel well and come down on Tuesday it shall make no difference, just you come — only, darling, I think if he is in the boat you should get out at Helensburgh. Well, beloved, you shall come to the gate (you know it) and wait till I come. And then, oh happiness, won't I kiss you, my love, my own sweet Emile, my husband dear. I don't think there is any risk. Well, Tuesday, 6th May. The gate, half-past ten. You understand, dear. I hope you are well—no cold. Take care of yourself. I have nothing new to tell you. I have been rather busy all this week. I shall expect you to have a letter for me. The weather is so fine. I have been a great deal out this week, looking after outdoor arrangements. I have got a new employment—the 'hen yard.' I go there every morning. You can fancy me every morning at ten o'clock seeing the hens being fed and feeding my donkey. I don't get on very fast with it—I fear it had little affection—do for it what I shall it only appears to know me and come to me when I call. My beloved Emile, I feel so delighted at the idea of seeing you that I cannot write. I hope you will be able to tell me that you shall get married in September. Darling, I love you and shall remain true for ever. Nothing shall cause me to break my vows to you. As you say, 'we are man and wife.' So we are, my pet. We shall, I trust, for ever remain so. It shall be the happiest day of my life that day that unites us never more to be parted. I trust and pray we shall for ever remain happy and loving. But there is no fear of that, we are sure to do so, love—are we not? But I must stop, as P. wishes me to go and read the papers to him—it is eleven o'clock night. So if I don't write any more, forgive me, love. Beloved of my soul, a fond embrace, a dear kiss till we meet. We shall have more than one love, dearest. From thy own ever devoted and loving wife, thine for ever,

"Mimi."

"1856. 14th June.

"My own beloved husband,—I trust to God that you got home safe, and were not much the worse for being out. Thank you, my love, for coming so far to see your Mimi. It is truly a pleasure to see you, my Emile. Beloved, if we did wrong last night it was in the excitement of our love. Yes, beloved, I did truly love you with my soul. I was happy, it was a pleasure to be with you. Oh, if only we could have remained, never more to have parted. But we must hope the time will come. I must have been very stupid to you last night. But everything goes out of my head when I see you, my darling, my love. I often think I must be very, very stupid in your eyes. You must be disappointed with me. I wonder you like me in the least. But I trust and pray the day may come when you shall like me better. Beloved, we shall wait till you are quite ready. I shall see and speak to Jack on Sunday. I shall consider about telling Mama. But I don't see any hope from her—I don't know her mind. You, of course, cannot judge of my parents. You know them not. I did not know (or I should not have done) that I caused you to pay extra postage for my stupid, cold letters—it shall not occur again. Darling Emile, did I seem cold to you last night? Darling, I love you. Yes, my own Emile, love you with my heart and soul. Am I not your wife? Yes, I am. And you may rest assured after what has happened I cannot be the wife of any other but dear, dear Emile. No, now it would be a sin. I am sorry you are going to lose your kind friends the Seivwrights. I am so glad when you have kind friends, for then I know you can go there of an evening and be happy. I often, often think of your long evenings by yourself. What a happy day de M—'s marriage day must have been. I have a regret that it was not ours—but the time shall pass away. I dread next winter. Only fancy, beloved, both of us in the same town and unable to write or see each other, it breaks my heart to think of it. Why, beloved, are we so unfortunate? I thank you very much for your dear, long letter. You are kind to me, love. I am sorry for your cold. You were not well last night, I saw you were not yourself. Beloved pet, take care of it. When may we meet (Oh that blot) again. A long time, is it not sad? I weep to think of it, to be separated thus—if you were far away, it would not be so bad, but to think you near me. I cannot see you when you come to Miss White's, as you could not be out so late. They cannot keep us from each other. No, that they never shall. Emile, beloved, I have sometimes thought you would like to go to Lima after we are married. Would that not do? Any place with you, pet. I shall always remember last night. Will we not often talk of our evening meetings after we are married. Why do you say in your letters—' If we are not married ? ' Beloved, have you a doubt but that we shall be married some day. I shall write to dear Mary soon. What would she say if she knew we were so intimate—lose all her good opinion of us—would she not ? My kind love to your dear sisters when you write. Tell me the names of your sisters. They shall be my sisters some day. I shall love them if they are like their dear brother, my dear husband. I know you can have little confidence in me. But, dear, I shall not flirt. I do not think it is right of me. I should only be pleasant to gentlemen. Free with none, my pet, in conversation but yourself. I shall endeavour to please you in this. Now, will you tell me at the end of the summer if you have heard anything about me flirting. Now, just you see how good your Mimi shall be. Pet, I see you smile and say, ' if she has a chance.' Try and trust me—love me. Beloved, adieu. I have your little note. What a kind letter Mary's. I won't come out in the serious light again. I must have been sad when I wrote her last letter. I am sorry for it. But you should not have given it to her. Adieu again, my husband. God bless you and make you well. And may you yet be very, very happy with your Mimi as your little wife. Kindest love, fond embrace, and kisses from thy own true and ever devoted Mimi, thy faithful wife."

But when her tone changed and her letters became cool and full of prevarications he wrote to her reproachfully, and it was, undoubtedly, his covert threats and angry criticisms which precipitated the tragedy. A specimen of his style will illustrate vividly the man and the environment of Madeleine Smith's first romance.

" In the first place, I did not deserve to be treated as you have done," he wrote on July 19th, 1855. " How you astonish me by writing such a note without condescending to explain the reasons why your father refuses his consent. He must have reasons, and I am not allowed to clear myself of accusations.

" I should have written to you before, but I preferred waiting until I got over the surprise your last letter caused me, and also to be able to write to you in a calm and a collected manner, free from any animosity whatever.

" Never, dear Madeleine, could I have believed you were capable of such conduct. I thought and believed you unfit for such a step. I believed you true to your word and to your honour. I will put questions to you which answer to yourself. What would you think if even one of your servants had played with any one's affections as you have done, or what would you say to hear that any of your lady friends had done what you have—or what am I to (think) of you now? What is your own opinion of yourself after those solemn vows you uttered and wrote to me. Shew your letters to any one, Madeleine. I don't care who, and if any find that I mislead you I will free you from all blame. I warned you repeatedly not to be rash in your engagement and vows to me, but you persisted in that false and deceitful flirtation, playing with affections you knew to be pure and undivided, and knowing at the same time that at a word from your father you would break off your engagement.

" You have deceived your father as you have deceived me. You never told him how solemnly you bound yourself to me, or if you had, for the honour of his daughter he could not have asked to break off an engagement as ours. Madeleine, you have truly acted wrong. May this be a lesson to you never to trifle with any one again. I wish you every happiness. I shall be truly happy to hear that you are happy with another. You desire and now you are at liberty to recognise me or cut me just as you wish—but I give you my word of honour I shall act always as a gentleman towards you. We may meet yet, as my intentions of going to Lima are now at an end. I would have gone for your sake. Yes, I would have sacrificed all to have you with me, and to leave Glasgow and your friends you detested so very much. Think what your father would say if I sent him your letters for a perusal. Do you think he would sanction your breaking your promises. No, Madeleine, I leave your conscience to speak for itself.

"I flatter myself he can only accuse me of a want of fortune. But he must remember he, too, had to begin the world with dark clouds round him.

"I cannot put it into my mind yet that you are at the bottom of all this."

That quarrel was patched up, but another broke out between them more than a year afterwards, and L'Angelier, stooping so low as to attempt to blackmail the unhappy girl into renewing their by now guilty relations, forced her to act the hypocrite in self-defence. She asked him to call late one night outside her bedroom window, and, so the prosecution alleged, when she got him there she gave him poisoned cocoa to drink, and a few hours later he was dead.

It is curious to reflect that had not Lord Justice-Clerk Hope written that letter of explanation and apology to which I have already referred, John Inglis would not have defended Madeleine Smith, for it was Hope who presided at her trial in the High Court of Edinburgh. Inglis was a man of his word, and nothing short of an apology would have induced him to appear before the man he was destined to succeed a year after the conclusion of the most romantic criminal trial in the annals of Scotland.

The speech that Inglis made on behalf of his client is now a classic. Every young barrister reads it at least once in his life, and it has been quoted times innumerable.

When Mr. Comrie Thomson defended A. J. Monson he used the opening words of Inglis' speech with telling effect, and, it is interesting to recall, it paved the way to an almost equally brilliant success, for Monson was acquitted.

It is hardly likely that there are any survivors of the large audience which heard the speech as Inglis delivered it, and, of course, there can be no comparison between reading a great speech and listening to it; yet there is something about this masterpiece of a great advocate which is compelling even in cold type.

There is not an unnecessary word—long as the speech is—and its perfect lucidity and clearness never hamper its eloquence. It is typical of Inglis. Like himself, it was brilliant, incisive, clear-cut, logical, and at the same time persuasive.

His old school-companion and friend, Moncrieff, Lord Advocate, led for the prosecution, and it was his duty to present his case coldly and dispassionately. It is never nice attacking a woman, especially a young and beautiful girl, and, although Moncrieff believed her to be guilty, it cannot be said that he took advantage of his position. The prosecution was unpopular, for, despite her sordid story, Madeleine Smith was a popular heroine, and every one's sympathies were with her. Inglis, therefore, had something in his favour, but, nevertheless, it was sheer personal merit which saved his client.

The verdict of the jury—thirteen to two for not proven—was without doubt a triumph for Inglis. Never before had an advocate done so much to earn fame. The Scottish Bar regarded the result as a great personal achievement on his part. He was already famous, but it was something to have made a speech which was to live for ever.

It was said at the time that Inglis attempted to write out his speech two days before he was to deliver it, but that realising he could not find words to express himself, decided to wait for inspiration until the moment he rose in court to make his final effort. He was armed with copious notes, but the most effective parts were purely spontaneous, and, in the circumstances, the address to the jury is a remarkable proof of his scholarship and his eloquence.

For a year after the acquittal of Madeleine Smith he was engrossed in political and social work. He was appointed Lord Advocate again in 1858, and Stamford returned him to the House of Commons, where, it was thought, he would gain fresh laurels. But the sudden death of the Lord Justice-Clerk afforded him an opportunity to take a position on the Bench in accordance with his abilities, and thus after a very short acquaintance with Parliament he became Lord Justice-Clerk of Scotland, and, to comply with the usual formality, took the title of Lord Glencorse, though he never used it.

In the stress of advocacy a barrister has to

think first of his client, and it is his duty to see only one side of a case. Inglis was never unfair either as prosecutor or defender, but naturally at the Bar there was little chance for the display of qualities such as impartiality, urbanity, and generosity to both sides which the Bench affords.

For nearly nine years he was Lord Justice-Clerk, presiding over many criminal trials which attracted attention in their time; and then, in February, 1867, he was installed as Lord Justice-General of Scotland and Lord President of the Court of Session, and he held this post for twenty-four years.

The great judge was one of the most popular men of his time. Everybody felt safe in his hands. His stately presence enhanced the dignity of the law without terrifying the wretches in the dock.

One of his earliest criminal trials as a judge was that of an Edinburgh jeweller named Milne. This person was an eccentric who was given to fits of temper bordering on madness. It was sufficient for an innocent stranger to brush against Milne in the street to convince the jeweller that he had been outrageously insulted. Anything which displeased him was said to be a conspiracy against his comfort. He had an idea that Edinburgh society did nothing but plan his ruin.

Equally puzzling were his periods of amiability. He was kind to children, and not ungenerous to those in distress. This was the somewhat complex character who murdered a friend, a man with whom he had been on the most intimate terms. Most madmen show cunning, but in the actual execution of the crime Milne displayed a contempt for privacy which seemed to indicate lunacy of an unusual kind. When he was arrested he talked about having his grievances remedied by the House of Commons. This outburst was followed by a confession of guilt, which he subsequently withdrew.

It was a peculiar case altogether, and it was lucky for the prisoner that Lord Justice-Clerk Inglis presided at his trial. The other judges were of the old school, and they only saw a murderer who deserved to be exterminated. Inglis, with his greater human sympathies, saw the man spoilt by failure to control a fiendish temper, and was sorry for him.

The only possible defence was a plea of lunacy, for the facts of the murder could not be disputed. The prosecution called for the death penalty nnd made great play with the prisoner's callousaess, but counsel for the defence, encouraged by the interest and sympathy of the presiding judge, confined himself to emphasising the prisoner's mental condition, although the other judges exhibited a certain restlessness which appeared to indicate incredulity.

Inglis summed up fairly and dispassionately, emphasising the principal arguments of the advocate for the defence, and his summing-up was so effective that, although the jury returned a verdict of guilty, it was by a majority of one only.

The law compelled Inglis to pass sentence of death, but he resolved that the sentence should not stand. Accordingly he wrote to the Home Secretary, with the result that the death sentence was commuted.

Some years after this case and when Inglis had completely forgotten all about it, the advocate who had defended Milne happened to refer to the trial in the presence of the Lord

President. Inglis remembered it at once, and asked after Milne. The advocate smiled grimly.

"I had a letter from him yesterday," he said, "in which he wasted a lot of ink cursing me for having saved his life."

It was Inglis who presided at the trial of Dr. Pritchard in 1865, and so eight years after the Madeleine Smith case he again found himself engaged in a *cause célèbre* which was the one topic of conversation of the time. Pritchard poisoned his wife and his mother-in-law, and was, in fact, one of the vilest of scoundrels and hypocrites ever seen in a criminal court. He was prosecuted by Solicitor-General Young, who had been Inglis' junior at the Madeleine Smith trial, and Rutherford Clark defended.

As the great judge listened to the evidence his mind no doubt often reverted to the 1857 trial, and he must have asked himself what he would have done had he been called upon to try and save Pritchard from the scaffold. There was much in common between the two trials. Both were poisoning cases, and only circumstantial evidence was available, and in each a vulgar intrigue was said to be the motive. But Pritchard's guilt was self-evident, and even the fairness of the Lord Justice-Clerk's charge to the jury could not prevent the general opinion that it crushed completely any hope the prisoner may have had of an acquittal.

In sentencing him to death Inglis did not harrow his feelings by dwelling upon the enormity of his crimes. There was only an exhortation to repentance after an expression of agreement with the jury, and then the black cap and the pronouncement of doom.

Pritchard was the last person to be publicly executed in Scotland, and as many as 100,000 persons witnessed his well-merited end. But Inglis was greatly shocked by the morbid taste of the public as displayed on this occasion, and he was one of the first to advise the Government to abolish public executions. It cannot be said that he alone brought about this reform so far as Scotland was concerned—England followed suit two or three years later—but undoubtedly his influence contributed a lot towards causing the Government of the day to make up their minds on the subject.

Outside the law Inglis had two causes at heart—religion and education. He was an elder at St. Andrew's for many years, and once when St. Giles' needed additional elders on a special occasion the elders sent a message to Inglis, then rich in years and honours, asking him to help them. The Lord President instantly responded, and at the next service the spectacle was witnessed of the frail judge serving communion bread amongst the pews.

Ever since his early days as a student at Glasgow University he had been anxious to further the cause of education in Scotland, and the first recognition of his public spirited efforts was his election as Lord Rector of King's College, Aberdeen, in 1857. Glasgow University elected him to a similar honour in 1865, and in 1869 he was selected to oppose Mr. Gladstone for the Chancellorship of Edinburgh University.

The Grand Old Man of politics was a year the senior of the Lord President, and just beginning his first notable premiership. The Edinburgh Liberals believed they were going to win, for the Prime Minister had all the resources and prestige of his great office behind him. Inglis, however, stood out as the greatest Scotsman of his generation, and, although the sphere of his activities was not so wide as Gladstone's, he was, after all, in his own country and amongst his own kin. Gladstone was defeated, and Lord President Inglis worthily maintained the traditions of the highest office which a university can bestow.

The election served to show the strong hold he had on the affections of his countrymen, as he had been selected as candidate when there were several graduates of Edinburgh available. It was feared, however, that Gladstone would defeat all but the very best, and so the Lord President was called in to save the Chancellorship for a native-born Scot resident in the capital.

Inglis used to say that the only place where he found both health and happiness was St. Andrews. He was, of course, a golfer, and a very enthusiastic one at that. In his younger days he took the game up, and then, owing to pressure of work, did not play for years, but when he had the leisure he started again, and he served a term as captain of the Royal and Ancient.

During the latter years of his life he generally put in three or four weeks every autumn at St. Andrews, going round the links daily, enthusiasm overcoming the disappointments caused by years increasing and skill decreasing. Tom Morris and he were great friends, and it was nothing unusual to see the two veterans discussing gravely the eternal subject of golf, more especially the chances of the leading Scots players at the ensuing open championship.

Great men have their hobbies. He would be a poor judge who found all he wanted in the law. Lord Brampton was devoted to dogs and racing; Lord Russell of Killowen to racing and cards; and Lord President Inglis to golf. Sir Henry Hawkins attained the great age of ninety, nine years longer than that of Inglis, who lived to within a day of the completion of his eighty-first year, while Russell died suddenly at sixty-eight. And yet Hawkins did not like the fresh air.

It was on the 20th of August, 1891, that Inglis died at his country house, Loganbank, Midlothian, after a long and fruitful life. The funeral of such a great man was fittingly marked by the attendance of all the judges at the service in St. Giles' Cathedral, an unprecedented honour, but one of which the greatest of Scottish judges was certainly worthy.

CHAPTER VI

Lord Chief Justice Coleridge

Three generations of the Coleridge family have given judges to the High Court, a record of success in the legal profession without parallel.

In 1835 Sir John Taylor Coleridge was promoted to the Bench, and his elder son, after serving as Chief Justice of the Common Pleas for seven years, was appointed Lord Chief Justice in 1880. To-day the latter's eldest son, the present Lord Coleridge, is a judge of the King's Bench Division.

John Duke Coleridge, the Lord Chief Justice, was born in 1820, a year which saw his father make headway at the Bar. The boy was sent to Eton and later to Oxford, where his personality was greater than his success as a scholar.

Young Coleridge was tall and distinguished-looking, and always fully conscious of his importance. During his stay at Eton his father became a judge, and, thanks to that and the eminence conferred on the family by the literary achievements of Samuel Taylor Coleridge, the schoolboy was an object of interest to his fellow-pupils long before it was known that he was a ready and eloquent speaker.

He was prematurely grave and dignified, but if he was respectful to his superiors, he demanded similar treatment from those he considered inferior to him, and in his opinion there were many such. However, he made plenty of friends at Oxford, and after rejecting a suggestion that he should enter the church, he studied for the Bar, and was called in November, 1846. With his father on the Bench and a host of influential friends, there was never any fear that Coleridge would not succeed. In addition to his undoubted abilities, he had innumerable well-wishers, but all he required was a chance, and from the day he got that he never required any one's interest.

When Coleridge became a fully-fledged barrister he was one of the tallest and handsomest men of his time. Standing six feet three, with clear cut features and a dignified carriage, he attracted attention at once, and his eloquence was compelling.

It is of interest to recall the fact that, after joining the Bar, one of his rivals and greatest friends was Sir John Karslake, who was three inches taller than he was. The two men were engaged in friendly rivalry for years, but just when Karslake shot ahead and became Solicitor-General, Coleridge overtook him, ascended the Bench, and Karslake, threatened with blindness, had to retire from his profession.

It was a murder trial that raised Coleridge's reputation above the restricted prestige he had already earned on the western circuit.

A tax-collector in the parish of Clayhidon, on the borders of Somerset and Devon, was murdered by two labourers, and the young barrister, fighting a hopeless cause, made such an eloquent and moving speech on behalf of the accused that from that moment he was recognised as one of the orators of his profession.

Briefs were plentiful, and Parliament, office, and the Bench became certainties. And if ever a man enjoyed success it was John Duke

Coleridge. In 1861 he took "silk," and four years later was elected Member of Parliament for Exeter.

Coleridge described Constance Kent as the most interesting and extraordinary client he ever had, and her story is certainly a very sensational and pathetic one. When he acted as her counsel he was not aware that she was a great grand-daughter of George III, a fact that was revealed years later.

The murder of Francis Saville Kent, a boy of four, on June 29th, 1860, created a great sensation, and divided the public as no other crime has ever done. At least six persons were suspected, and each one had his or her champions, who were all fiercely partisan until the day came when the guilty one confessed, and the great mystery was unexpectedly solved.

Road Hill House was a pleasant roomy building on the borders of Wiltshire and four miles from Frome in Somerset, and at the time of the murder it was occupied by Mr. Samuel Saville Kent, a Government Inspector of Factories, his wife and their children.

Mr. Kent had been married first to a lady who had died insane, leaving him four children—three girls and a boy. Constance Kent was the youngest of the girls, the boy being one year her junior. But soon after his first wife's death, Mr. Kent had married again, proposing to his daughters' governess, Miss Pratt. This lady was kind enough to her step-children; in fact, they all liked her; Constance was one of her bridesmaids at her wedding, but as the child was only nine, this cannot be taken to signify that she approved of her father's second matrimonial venture.

But from all accounts when the family removed to Road Hill House, there was no real unhappiness. The children got on well together, and the second Mrs. Kent treated them all alike. Her husband left to her the entire management of his household, and she ruled it firmly and wisely, though, now and then, she allowed her tongue to out-run her discretion, a common failing, but one which in this case was destined to have tragic consequences.

The germ of the subsequent tragedy first developed in the early summer of 1856. Mrs. Kent was in a delicate state of health, and Constance, a high-spirited girl of twelve, did something to offend her. Momentarily losing her temper, the step-mother angrily remarked to the child that her conduct seemed to indicate that she had inherited her mother's madness. Constance did not reply, and the incident appeared to have ended as quickly as it had begun, but Mrs. Kent did not understand the peculiar temperament of the child. Constance had not forgotten the poor, affectionate mother who had suffered so grievously before her death, and in that moment she began to hate the woman whom her father had set to reign over them. She brooded over the insult Mrs. Kent had flung at her, and she never forgot the contemptuous reference to her still lamented mother.

No one, however, noticed the change in the girl. Mrs. Kent was as kind as ever, and on the surface the family appeared to be very happy. One day, however, Constance and her brother, William, were missing. They were to return to school the next morning, and it was assumed that their disappearance was due to a natural dislike to exchanging the society of the pleasant country house for the discipline of a school.

All available hands were pressed into the search, and, finally, the runaways were found in Bath, where Constance was discovered dressed as a boy. She readily confessed that she had donned an old suit of her brother's after persuading him to accompany her. William was quite content. It was Constance who was the rebel. Her object, she said, was to leave England and make herself independent in one of the colonies. A remarkable adventure altogether for a girl of twelve, who proved her doggedness by covering the ten miles to Bath on foot.

There were, of course, many who sympathised with her. The general opinion was that it was all the fault of the "cruel step-mother." Stepmothers must be cruel if they wish to be conventional. The old legend was revived, and Constance Kent was the object of a great deal of pity, whilst her step-mother was censured undeservedly. Her own sisters, however, declared that Mrs. Kent was uniformly kind to them all, and the local gossip died down. A few weeks later Mrs. Kent gave birth to a son, who was christened Francis Saville.

The years passed by peacefully for the family. They were well-to-do, and had most of the comforts of life. Mr. Kent was an indulgent father, and his wife made no difference between her own children and those of the first Mrs. Kent. Naturally the babies received more attention, but they were petted by Constance and her sisters just as much as by their mother. It was apparently a united, happy family with not a care in the world, for there can be no doubt of the fact that, save for the one lapse into bad taste already cited, Mrs. Kent was a model step-mother. She had tact, and was good-natured, and there was some excuse for her in the state of her health when she made the mistake of referring slightingly to the mother of her four step-children.

Such was the condition of affairs on that June day in 1860, when the terrible tragedy occurred. Road Hill House by now contained a dozen inmates, surely a sufficient precaution against a tragedy happening from within. Mr. Kent was at home, and only two persons had separate bedrooms. These were Constance and her brother William. The two youngest children had their cots in the nurse's room, and Francis, now nearly four years old, slept in the one furthest from the door, the faithful nurse on guard, as it were, between him and any intruder. The night of June 29th passed and Elizabeth Gough, the nurse, woke up, rubbed her eyes and looked round the room. The baby girl was fast asleep, but Master Francis' cot was empty. The nurse glanced at the clock and saw that it was just five.

"Mistress has taken him into her own bed," she murmured sleepily and, turning over, dozed off again. She slept for two hours, and then rose and dressed. Knocking at Mrs. Kent's door, she asked if the boy was ready to be dressed. To her astonishment Mrs. Kent asked her what she meant. The nurse explained that she had missed the child at five, but had decided that he was with his mother.

In an instant Mrs. Kent was out of bed and dressed, and every one in the house was raised and questioned. There was no sign of little Francis anywhere, and Mr. Kent, after giving instructions that every square inch of the garden was to be searched, drove to Trowbridge, three miles away, to notify the police of the loss of his son.

Before the police arrived, however, the child's dead body was discovered. Two of the searchers had found it in an old and disused outhouse. The child's throat had been cut, but there was no sign of the weapon, and no clue.

The inquest excited great interest and led to a prolonged inquiry. Constance and other members of the family gave evidence, and the verdict returned as one of wilful murder against some person or persons unknown, the coroner adding that the day would come when the murderer would be brought to justice.

The conduct of the inquest, however, caused general dissatisfaction, and the papers commented severely on the proceedings. The whole country was naturally throbbing with an intense desire to see the guilty person punished. Everybody's sympathies were aroused by the description of the crime—the innocent child taken from his cot at dead of night to be foully murdered. There was a general cry for revenge Every mother and father voiced it. The mystery was debated everywhere, and several persons were mentioned as likely to be in possession of the truth concerning the death of Francis Saville Kent. His father was denounced for not having given evidence at the inquest. There were those who suspected the mother, but these were very few. The step-sisters of the deceased were mentioned, but amid all the turmoil and excitement Constance was seldom referred to.

The authorities, roused by the universal desire to punish the murderer, decided to commission Scotland Yard to help the local police, and one of the cleverest and shrewdest detectives was sent down to Road Hill House.

Inspector Whicher was a man with an original

mind, which often took him beyond the more conventional deductions of his colleagues. He had " theories " and " ideas," and was, in fact, a good specimen of the " Sherlock Holmes " in real life. Certainly, there were plenty of theories to be found at Road Hill House, but little else. On the face of it there was no earthly reason why anyone should have murdered the rosy-cheeked boy of four. The Kent family had no enemies. They were all popular. And if it was decided that the criminal was a member of the family, which one could it be? The elder step-sisters were of good character, quiet and affectionate. Constance, now sixteen years of age, was a typical schoolgirl, affectionate, too, and devoted to her relations. She had often nursed little Frank before his tragic death, and there was no doubt that the child had loved her.

While Whicher was working on the case an attempt was being made in London to get the inquest proceedings quashed and a special commission appointed to enquire all over again into the whole affair. The Lord Chief Justice, however, refused the request, and now everything depended on the detective.

It is doubtful if Whicher had a single clue of real value. The weapon had never been found, and the flannel vest and tiny nightdress the child had been wearing when murdered were of no value. But after he had eliminated several " probables " from his mind he came to the first of the possibles, Constance Kent, and he built up a series of theories linking her with the crime. His conclusion was that Constance Kent was the murderer, and he hazarded the opinion that she had taken Francis from his cot, carried him out of the house by stepping out of the drawing room window with the child in her arms, and had cut his throat in the outhouse. He further surmised that she wore a nightdress at the time, which must have been stained, as the body of her victim had bled profusely. Against the latter theory was the evidence of the doctor attending the family that he had examined the girl's nightdresses and had found no bloodstains. But Inspector Whicher suggested that the three nightdresses which the doctor had seen did not include the one Constance had worn when committing the crime. There was a clothes basket in the girl's bedroom, and this would contain a used nightdress, which, he said, Constance had abstracted and substituted for the blood-stained garment. If this theory was wrong, he added, there was the possibility that when the doctor had examined the three nightdresses the bloodstained one, having recently been washed, would not then show any signs of blood, but that later when quite dry it would, and that having, in the usual course, been thrown into the clothes basket to be sent to the wash, Constance had taken it and burnt it.

Convinced that his version was correct, Inspector Whicher startled the country by arresting Constance and taking her to Devizes Gaol, and less than a month after the murder she made her appearance before the magistrates at Frome.

The arrest served to add fuel to the fiery interest taken in the affair by the public. The whole country had been looking for the murderer, and every one was desperately anxious to avenge Francis Kent's death, but the sixteen-year-old step-sister in the dock created something of a reaction.

It seemed incredible that a young and pretty girl could be a murderer. Few could believe her capable of such a fearful crime. Where was there in any civilised country a girl of sixteen who could rise in the darkness and loneliness of midnight and deliberately convey her baby brother into an outhouse and cut his throat? It was absurd, and from the beginning Inspector Whicher had to face a considerable amount of criticism.

It was said that he had simply arrested the girl to save his own face; that Scotland Yard felt it must arrest somebody or look extremely foolish, and of course Inspector Whicher's "theories" were subjected to ridicule, not only by the public but by his own colleagues.

There was only one hearing before the magistrates, Constance being represented by an eminent London barrister. Inspector Whicher gave his evidence and expounded his theories. The evidence was, of course, purely circumstantial. No one could have witnessed the deed, and if the murderer was convicted, it would have to be on circumstantial evidence alone.

The Scotland Yard detective's theories were too much for the Bench, and the abstracted nightdress idea was held to be too much like an extract from a popular detective romance to command or deserve respect. The accused's counsel would not treat the prosecution seriously. He scarcely defended; he only demanded in the name of Justice that his young and innocent client should be discharged at once and restored to her family. He protested angrily against an adjournment, ridiculing the evidence of dissensions in the family, and pointing out that if the murderer was a member of the Kent family it was more likely to be one of the older children of the late Mrs. Kent than this young girl in the dock.

The prosecution made a valiant attempt to prove that the children of the first wife hated those of the reigning Mrs. Kent. As is usual, there was much evidence advanced on both sides; and doubtless, as in all families, it was very easy to prove that there had been occasional quarrels. But step-mothers have not a monopoly of family quarrels, and whatever was advanced in support of the prosecution in this respect was greatly discounted by the sworn statement on behalf of the prisoner.

The counsel for the defence gained the day, and, probably, for the first and only time in the history of crime an accused murderer was discharged on the occasion of the first appearance before the magistrates. The acquittal of Constance Kent was received with applause, and for a time she was something of a heroine.

Inspector Whicher returned to London a bitterly disappointed man. All his grand theories had been smashed by ridicule. The papers laughed at him, and fellow-detectives who did not believe in his "theories" chaffed him unmercifully. Yet he had been correct in every detail! His feat was, in fact, one of the greatest achieved by a detective in real life. Without a clue he had traced the murderer and had evolved the complete story of her doings on the night of her crime.

The release of Constance Kent made the country more anxious than ever for the arrest of the murderer, and the interest increased. Rumours were manufactured in abundance, and half a dozen arrests were reported, only to be contradicted.

Then the nurse, Elizabeth Gough, was taken into custody, and once more the Road Case, as it was called, occupied the attention of a magisterial Bench. For a week the nurse sat in court listening to the evidence for and against her. She protested her innocence volubly and excitedly, in marked contrast to the quiet behaviour Constance Kent had shown in a similar predicament. But, of course, there was no direct proof that the woman had murdered her charge, and she, too, was acquitted, and the Road Mystery became more mysterious than ever.

It was still felt that something must be done, and a local magistrate conducted another inquiry on his own account. It was a comic affair, and it died a natural death, choked by thousands of anonymous letters, wild statements, and distorted evidence.

Soon after her ordeal Constance was sent to a convent in France to complete her education. In 1863 she returned to England, and was placed in St. Mary's Home, Brighton, an Anglican Sisterhood, under the charge of the curate of the parish of St. Paul's Church there. The crime was still a topic of conversation, but by now no one dreamed that it would ever be solved. Four inquiries had been held—the inquest; the prosecution of Constance Kent and Elizabeth Gough, and the unofficial proceedings conducted by Mr. Saunders—and nothing definite had resulted. There seemed no possible reason to expect that the murderer would be found when the unexpected happened with dramatic suddenness. Sir Thomas Henry, the Chief Magistrate at Bow Street, was informed by Superintendent Durking, of Scotland Yard, that Miss Constance Kent desired to surrender herself to him for the murder of Francis Saville Kent, and the very day Sir Thomas received the startling news the self-confessed murderer entered his private room at Bow Street, accompanied by Superintendent Durking and Chief Inspector Williamson, and there she handed to him the following statement in her own handwriting:

"I, Constance Kent, alone and unaided, on the night of June 29th, 1860, murdered at Road Hill House, Wiltshire, one Francis Saville Kent. Before the deed was done no one knew of my intention, nor afterwards of my guilt. No one assisted me in my crime, nor in the evasion of the discovery."

When the genuineness of her confession was realised she was removed to Trowbridge, as the crime had been committed in Wiltshire, and having been committed for trial she was examined by a mental specialist on behalf of the Government to see if she was suffering from a mental disease.

The specialist, Dr. Bucknill, issued at the prisoner's desire a full statement as to how she planned and carried out her awful crime, and that statement proved that it had not been a case of sudden temper, but a deliberately planned murder, carefully executed. The doctor's statement was:

"A few days before the murder she obtained possession of a razor from a green case in her father's wardrobe, and secreted this. This was the sole instrument which she used. She also secreted a candle with matches by placing them in the corner of the outhouse in the garden where the crime was committed. On the night of the murder she undressed herself and went to bed because she expected her sisters to visit her room. She lay awake watching until she thought that the household were all asleep, and soon after midnight she left her bedroom and went downstairs and opened the drawing room door and window shutters. She then went up into the nursery, withdrew the blanket from between the sheet and the counterpane, and placed it on the side of the cot. She then took the child from his bed and carried him downstairs, through the drawing room. She had on her nightdress and in the drawing room she put on her goloshes.

"Having the child in one arm, she raised the drawing room window with the other hand, went round the house and into the outhouse, lighted the candle, the child being wrapped in the blanket and still sleeping, and when the child was in this position she inflicted the wound in the throat.

"She went back to her bedroom, examined her nightdress and found only two spots of blood on it. These she washed out in the basin, and threw the water, which was but little discoloured, into the footpan in which she had washed her feet overnight. She took another of her nightdresses and got into bed. In the morning her nightdress had become dry where it had been washed. She folded it up and put it into the drawer. Her three nightdresses were examined by Mr. Foley and, she believes, by Mr. Parsons, the medical attendant of the family. She thought the blood stains were effectually washed out, but on holding the dress up to the light a day or two afterwards she found the stains were still visible. She secreted the dress, moving it from place to place, and she eventually burnt it in her own room, and put the ashes into the kitchen grate. It was about five or six days after the child's death that she burnt the nightdress. On the Saturday morning (the day after the crime) she cleaned the razor and replaced it unobserved in the case in the wardrobe. She abstracted the nightdress from the clothes basket when the housemaid went to fetch a glass of water.

"As regards the motive of her crime, it seems that although she entertained a great regard for the present Mrs. Kent, yet if any remark was at any time made which, in her opinion, was disparaging to any member of the first family, she treasured it up and determined to avenge it. She had no ill-will against the little boy, except as one of the children of her step-mother. She declared that both her father and her stepmother had always been kind to her personally, and the following is a copy of a letter which she adressed to Mr. Rodway, her solicitor, on this point while in prison awaiting her trial:

"'Sir,—It has been stated that my feelings for revenge were excited in consequence of cruel treatment. This is entirely false. I have received the greatest kindness from both the persons accused of subjecting me to it. I have never had any ill-will towards either of them on account of their behaviour to me, which has been very kind. I shall feel obliged if you will make use of this statement in order that the public may be undeceived on this point.'

"She told me that when the nursemaid was accused she had fully made up her mind to confess if the nurse had been convicted. She said that she had felt herself under the influence of the devil before she had committed the murder, but that she did not believe, and had not believed, that the devil had more to do with her crime than he had with any other wicked action. She had not said her prayers for a year before the murder, and not afterwards until she came to reside at Brighton. She said that the circumstance which revived religious feelings in her mind was thinking about receiving the sacrament when confirmed."

This was the specialist's report of her own statement, and the accused confirmed it. Of course, it was not published until after the trial had taken place.

When she was tried at the assizes at Salisbury on the 20th July, 1865, just five years had elapsed since the murder. It could not be a lengthy trial because the prisoner pleaded guilty, but the courthouse was packed, and thousands struggled in vain to gain an entry. Constance Kent was defended by Coleridge, and the presiding judge was Mr. Justice Willes.

There was very little to be done beyond hearing how the prisoner had confessed to the Rev. Mr. Wagner, the curate of the Brighton church, and how she had insisted upon travelling to London and giving herself up. He had not, he said, influenced her either way, because he believed that the girl would do what was right. During her stay at St. Mary's Home she had become deeply religious and her conscience would not permit her to rest until she had made whatever reparation she could for the murder of her poor little step-brother. That was her only motive now, and if her eminent counsel made a plea for mercy she asked for none.

The only verdict possible was returned by the jury, and the girl of twenty-one was sentenced to death. During his final remarks Mr. Justice

Willes was overcome, and burst into tears, and the sight of the venerable judge's emotion broke down the prisoner's composure and she sobbed unrestrainedly.

But there was never any fear that the sentence would be carried into execution, and soon after the moving scene in court the convicted prisoner was reprieved and ordered to undergo penal servitude for life. Thus a few months over twenty-one, just when life ought to have held all its pleasures and attractions for her, the walls of the prison closed round her, and she was faced with a life-time of misery. The best years of her life were spent in penal servitude, but she gave no trouble and never complained.

At Portland Prison she assisted in the decoration of the chapel, and the beautiful mosaics she was responsible for are still pointed out to visitors as the work of the murderer of Francis Saville Kent.

She was eventually released on ticket-of-leave after serving twenty years. She had entered prison a young woman; she left it prematurely old, a woman of forty-one who had escaped one trial for murder, but had eventually surrendered herself to justice because of an uneasy conscience. When she returned to the world she was fortunate enough to find that she had been forgotten, and she was able to retire quietly and pass the remaining years of her life in comparative peace.

Except for the Tichborne trial, the most remarkable civil cause with which Coleridge was connected as counsel was the action for libel brought by Risk Allah against the proprietors of the *Daily Telegraph.*

Risk Allah was an Assyrian, who married a wealthy English widow. This lady had a nephew, Charles Readley, and when she died somewhat suddenly it was found that by her will she had left everything to her husband except the sum of five thousand pounds, which was to be held in trust for her nephew.

Young Readley lived with Risk Allah, and the two men travelled about extensively until the morning Readley, failing to answer knocks on his door at the hotel at Spa, was discovered to be dead in bed, having apparently shot himself. It was known that he had got into debt, and that his engagement to a young lady had been imperilled by his conduct, but as his uncle by marriage, Risk Allah, benefited to the extent of five thousand pounds by his death, and as the weapon with which Readley had come by his wounds was found in a position which suggested murder, Risk Allah was arrested and charged with the crime. A Brussels jury, however, acquitted him after a patient hearing.

The *Daily Telegraph* thereupon published comments on Risk Allah's character, which caused him to bring the action, and in spite of Coleridge's keen cross-examination of the plaintiff, followed up by a very clever speech, the plaintiff was awarded nine hundred and sixty pounds damages by the jury. Any one studying a full report of the case will be struck by many curious facts which were never explained, and certainly there was more than mere suspicion to justify a common belief that young Readley had been murdered.

When the Tichborne claimant tried to enforce his rights he was anxious to have Mr. Henry Hawkins, Q.C., for his leading counsel, and he was accordingly retained. But the famous lawyer asked to be released, and he was afterwards brought in on the other side, with Coleridge as his junior. However, in 1868, Coleridge became Solicitor-General, and, therefore, Hawkins' senior at the Bar, and he led for the defence at the trial before Chief Justice Bovill, which resulted in the defeat of the plaintiff.

Coleridge did not shine at the cross-examination of Arthur Orton, but his closing speech, which occupied twenty-six days, was probably the very finest he delivered in the course of his career at the Bar. It did more than anything else to smash the claimant.

Chief Justice Bovill did not long survive the longest trial on record, and when he died in 1873 Coleridge was given the post of Chief Justice of the Common Pleas, which, at the decease of Sir Alexander Cockburn in 1880, was exchanged for that of Lord Chief Justice of England. He was now in his element. For all his success at the Bar, Coleridge was more at home on the Bench. He was dignified and urbane, and his presence was majestic.

No other Chief Justice looked the part better than he did, and the charm and richness of his voice were in keeping with his high office. It was said that he could read a page out of Bradshaw's Railway Guide and make it interesting.

Thus at the age of sixty the friend of Archbishop Temple, Matthew Arnold, Tennyson, Cardinal Newman, and many other famous men, was occupying the highest non-political position on the Bench, and for fourteen years he was one of the most prominent men in the country.

Lord Coleridge—he was raised to the peerage in 1874—did not confine himself to his judicial duties. He was fond of making speeches, and in his anxiety to be all things to all men he was occasionally just a trifle too unctuous. Now and then his affected humility was irritating, but it was quite harmless, and the sincerity of his motive was never in doubt.

A specimen of his style and of his manner is afforded by his speech when responding for the University of Oxford at a banquet given to celebrate the opening of a new college hall. Archbishop Tait had responded for Baliol College, and Lord Chief Justice Coleridge, speaking for the university, said in the course of his remarks :

" The most reverend prelate, in spite of his far more exalted position and infinitely superior eloquence, has on this memorable occasion only been called upon to respond for a part, while I, in every respect his inferior, who cannot claim to excel in a single one of the accomplishments with which he is so lavishly endowed, I, my lords and gentlemen, have been asked to respond for Oxford as a whole, and, my lords and gentlemen, what a whole Oxford is ! "

It took him a little time to understand the reason for the laughter that ensued.

Once he was sitting with a brother judge when a barrister handed to him a slip of paper containing the name of the latest appointment to the Bench. The promoted counsel was obnoxious to both judges, and Coleridge's colleague criticised the new judge in very strong language.

When he had finished the Lord Chief Justice turned to him with a grave face, and remarked in a melodious tone :

" I am not addicted to expressions of that kind myself, but would you mind saying it again ! "

It was characteristic of Coleridge that he should do his swearing by proxy.

But in the course of his duties as a judge he never shrank from the dirty linen which was so often exhibited before him. In common with all barristers who reach the Bench, he had defended and prosecuted murderers, and as a judge he tried them. Some of the most amazing criminal trials of the nineteenth century took place before him, although he did not imitate his great predecessor, Cockburn, and endeavour to reserve all the interesting cases for himself.

In the annals of the sea there can scarcely be a more dramatic romance than that of the last voyage of the *Mignonette*, which, after a series of extraordinary adventures, ended in a sordid trial for murder.

On the 19th of May, 1884, the *Mignonette* sailed from Southampton for Australia, but in the following July, and when sixteen hundred miles from the Cape, it foundered in a terrible storm. The captain, Thomas Dudley; the mate, Edwin Stephens; a seaman named Brooks, and a boy, Richard Parker, managed to escape in an open boat, but without any provisions. For nearly twenty days the boat drifted with its starving crew, and the captain, seeing that death by starvation faced them all, proposed that they should cast lots to select one of their number to be killed, so that the others might eat and live. He was willing to take his chance in the ghoulish lottery, but the seaman, Brooks, opposed this cannibalistic proposal, and it was abandoned. However, after another night of horror the captain, half-crazy through suffering, killed the boy, Richard Parker, and the survivors devoured the body. Shortly afterwards the boat was picked up by the German barque

Montezuma, and the three men were taken to Falmouth. When Brooks told the story of the death of Parker the captain and mate were instantly arrested and charged with wilful murder.

It was a sensational affair, and was widely discussed. The problem Captain Dudley had been faced with was a unique one. It simply amounted to this: When four persons are confronted by death are they justified in taking one life to save the other three? It was admitted that had not the captain killed the boy all of them would have perished.

The trial took place at Exeter, and when the facts had been affirmed the case was remitted to the Queen's Bench, where Lord Chief Justice Coleridge presided with the other judges to decide whether Dudley and Stephen were deserving of death.

Coleridge's judgment was against the accused. He held that the law of England permitted no alternative to the death sentence when murder was proved, but it was generally known that the sentence would not be carried out. The captain and the mate were reprieved, kept in confinement for six months, without hard labour, and then released.

A remarkable society case of outstanding interest was the action Lonsdale *v.* Edmund Yates. Yates, the brilliant journalist and author, was the editor of the *World*, and in the early 'eighties he attacked Lord Lonsdale in its columns—an attack which made it necessary for the earl to charge him with criminal libel. The contest was fought with great bitterness on both sides, and when Yates lost, and was sentenced to four months' imprisonment, he appealed to a higher court to overrule the decision given by a jury under Lord Coleridge's direction. But again the journalist lost, and he had to serve his term in gaol.

It is more than probable that Lord Coleridge was never on a race-course in his life and that he disliked card playing, yet he presided over two of the greatest trials arising out of gambling. The first was the action for libel brought by Charles Wood, the famous jockey, against Mr. Cox, who charged him in a sporting paper with having on two occasions "pulled" the horse "Success." It was, of course, a very damaging statement to make, and if proved would have meant the end of Wood's career on the turf.

Nine days were occupied by the case, and the Lord Chief Justice learned more about horse racing than he had ever imagined he could be taught. Owners, jockeys, bookmakers, and society leaders gave evidence, and the court was crowded daily with all sorts and conditions of turfites. Coleridge, the dignified, scholarly, and, it must be confessed, sanctimonious judge, listened without revealing any amazement to a jargon he scarcely understood. But a great jockey's honour was at stake, and, despite his abhorrence of all forms of gambling, he was impartial and judicious.

The result of the protracted hearing was that Charles Wood was held to have ridden "Success" fairly, but because there was so much unsatisfactory evidence on both sides the judge, after commending the jury's award of a farthing to the plaintiff, would not give the winner his costs.

There was some talk at the conclusion of the action about the unfairness of having a sporting case tried by a non-sporting judge, but it can be said that Coleridge brought to the affair an open mind. A judge with a leaning towards the turf might have taken sides early on in the case, but Coleridge was drawn neither way, and his conduct was decidedly impartial. No one ever suspected him of being guided or influenced by his prejudices when Lord Chief Justice.

The second *cause célèbre* connected with gambling was even more notorious, and it is now known in history as "The Baccarat Case." No murder trial ever created the talk and agitation that this attempt on the part of a distinguished army officer to clear his name did. Members of the royal family were dragged into it; questions were asked in Parliament, and every name connected with it was blackened indiscriminately, although from first to last there had been only one culprit.

The story is a simple one and very sad. In September, 1890, a small house party assembled at Tranby Croft, near Doncaster, the residence of Mr. Arthur Wilson, the shipowner. The chief guest was the Prince of Wales (afterwards King Edward VII), and the others included General Owen, the Earl of Coventry, and Colonel Sir William Gordon Cumming, all three intimate friends of the prince, the last-named a soldier with a record of which he was justly proud.

As usual cards were played, and amongst the games indulged in was baccarat. Considering the wealth and position of the parties concerned it cannot be said that they gambled extravagantly, but for some unaccountable reason Sir William Gordon Cumming played unfairly. He was said to have been seen cheating by a young officer, who was one of the party, and that this person, hesitating to bring so serious a charge against a gentleman of the baronet's standing in society, waited until the evidence of his eyes could be corroborated by a friend. Together they watched Sir William on the following night, when according to their story the baronet again cheated.

After this they had no option but to inform the Prince of Wales, who was, of course, greatly distressed at the terrible lapse of his old friend. However, it was too serious a matter to pass over, and Sir William was summoned to an informal "court-martial," at which the Prince of Wales pronounced sentence. He decided that on Sir William giving a written promise that he would never touch a card again they would all keep his secret. That promise was given, and the house party broke up. The prince returned to London, and within a few days the parties concerned were scattered over England and Scotland.

But the secret was not kept. Some one gave it away. Sir William Gordon Cumming found that he was being given the cold shoulder in London. Men looked askance at him in his clubs. Vague rumours reached him, rumours which grossly magnified the truth. It was said that the Prince of Wales had actually caught him cheating and had denounced him to his face in the midst of their mutual friends. It is not astonishing that the baronet's position became untenable, and when he understood that houses which had once been thrown open to him gladly were now closed against him he felt that he must do something to save his name and reputation.

Accordingly he issued an action for libel against Mr. and Mrs. Lycett Green (the latter was a daughter of Mr. Wilson) and other fellow-guests at Tranby Croft, and he retained Sir

Edward Clarke as his leading counsel. Defendant secured the services of Sir Charles Russell, and it was only in keeping with the importance of the case that the Lord Chief Justice of England should try the action himself.

Whoever advised Sir William to bring the case into court did him a bad turn, because the attempt to clear his character failed, mainly owing to the magnanimity of the Prince of Wales, who, knowing that the defendants would be greatly handicapped if he did not give evidence, volunteered to enter the witness-box and tell what he knew of the deplorable affair.

As Sir William's case was based on the statement that he had been coerced into signing what was practically a confession, it was necessary for the defendants to prove that he had actually cheated.

The intimation that the Prince of Wales was going to be a witness instantly made the baccarat case notorious all over the world. Competition to secure a seat in the court was phenomenal. Bribery was resorted to without effect, and the first man into the gallery when the trial opened had spent the night waiting outside the door.

Lord Coleridge was the right judge for what was essentially a society affair. He could be relied upon to do justice to all concerned, and, while extending a respectful welcome to the prince on his appearance as a witness, he did not forget that, as Lord Chief Justice, he was the representative of the Queen, and, therefore, supreme within the jurisdiction of the court. Lord Coleridge was a popular figure in society himself, and although, when visiting America, he had, in his anxiety to win the plaudits of the crowd, uttered fulsome praises of American democracy to the disparagement of Great Britain, yet at heart he was anything but democratic. He liked society, and made no secret of the fact.

In the witness-box the Prince of Wales stated that he thought he was doing an old friend a very great service by letting him off so lightly. Any one else would have been publicly denounced and expelled from society, but because the baronet had risked his life for his country, and because it was unbelievable that he had been himself when he had fallen from his usual high standard of honour, the prince had offered to save him from social ruin if he would promise not to gamble again.

Sir Edward Clarke had a delicate and difficult task in cross-examining the prince, but he managed to do his best for his client and at the same time offer no disrespect to the heir to the throne. But Sir Edward could not demolish hard facts. A brilliant speech was matched by Sir Charles Russell's reply, and the jury found for the defendants, with costs. This meant that Sir William Gordon Cumming was branded as a cheat before the whole world, but his counsel never ceased to believe in his innocence.

There were many sequels to the trial, and the prince was inundated with anonymous letters of the abusive kind. Several obscure members of the House of Commons sought to discredit him by initiating a debate on his failure to submit Sir William's case to his commander-in-chief, but there was no debate, because his Royal Highness admitted that he had committed an error of judgment in not doing so. However, time healed many of the wounds caused by the unfortunate scandal, and it was not very long ere most of the prince's critics realised that they had done him an injustice. As for Lord Coleridge, he came out of the ordeal very well, wisely confining himself to the judicial aspects of the affair, and taking scrupulous care not to be tempted into offering an opinion of it outside his court.

Ten years previous to the baccarat case Lord Coleridge sat at Maidstone to try Percy Lefroy, the murderer of Mr. Isaac Gold. The story of that crime is very well known, because railway murders have been very infrequent in Great Britain, and the few have created enormous interest. Lefroy's crime was the second of its kind, and, owing to his success in evading arrest for a few days, the popular excitement was intense.

Lefroy was a ne'er-do-well who seems to have lived by his wits, and, as his wits were poor, he was generally penniless. There is no doubt that he boarded the Brighton train that June day in 1881 with the intention of robbing some prosperous-looking person and adding murder to the crime of robbery if he met with any resistance.

His victim proved to be a retired merchant, who was in the habit of journeying weekly to London to collect certain moneys due to him. Lefroy attacked him suddenly, but the old man fought desperately for his life, and when the murderer had flung him from the train he was covered with blood. However, Lefroy got free of the railway officials at Brighton, and, although two policemen were deputed to see him to Wallington, they never thought of taking any precaution to shadow him, so that if subsequently wanted he might easily be secured. This was all the more extraordinary as the body of Mr. Gold had been found a few hours after

Lefroy had told his story to the railway officials.

But, of course, once the hue and cry was raised the murderer had no chance of escaping justice. He hid in an East End garret for some days in a condition of starvation and terror, and when at last he betrayed his whereabouts by an indiscreet telegram to an acquaintance he was pounced upon by detectives and taken to Scotland Yard. There he was provided with food, which he ate ravenously.

Lefroy was probably about the vainest murderer who has appeared in the dock. When the police superintendent asked him if he required anything specially for his trial, he answered—" I wish you'd let me have the pawn-ticket for my dress clothes, as I would like to redeem them and wear them in court." Denied this, he devoted himself to the sole remaining proof of his gentility, a silk hat, and throughout the trial he took particular care of it, and when the Attorney-General was pressing the facts which were to hang him, the murderer scarcely paid any attention, giving all his time to the safety and well-being of his hat !

Montague Williams defended Lefroy, and in a brilliant speech came as near acquittal as any one could have expected. It was the opinion of Sir Henry James, Q.C., M.P., the prosecuting Attorney-General, that the jury would give the prisoner the benefit of the doubt, but Williams, who knew Lord Chief Justice Coleridge, was not convinced.

" He has to sum up yet," he said, shaking his head, " and I am afraid that he will settle Lefroy's chance."

While it cannot be said that Coleridge's charge to the jury was unfair, yet it was a fact that as he calmly and dispassionately reviewed the evidence he slowly but surely crushed the defence to atoms. The judge was at his best on this occasion, and in a long summing-up there was no point of importance which he missed. Lefroy, confident of success, listened to the opening with an amused and careless smile, but as the judge proceeded the jauntiness left the prisoner, the smile died away, and his expression became anxious and strained. He shifted in his seat, glanced uneasily around the court, and even forgot his hat. Fear was proving too much for his vanity. There could have been no greater contrast than that presented by the imposing presence of the judge and the thin-chested, shrivelling wretch in the dock.

After the inevitable verdict of guilty the judge passed sentence of death. Lefroy swayed in the dock, and was about to collapse, when he succeeded in pulling himself together. Then he turned towards the jury, and in a shrill voice cried, "Some day you will learn, when too late, that you have murdered me." Before his execution he confessed his guilt.

These cases are, of course, only a selection from amongst a score and more, for the Lord Chief Justice never neglected his duties, although tempted by many appeals from social, educational, and philanthropic bodies for the aid of his eloquence at their principal festivals. He was very strong physically, and although in 1894 he had been nearly twenty-one years on the Bench, there was no reason to suppose that he would not survive that year.

On 2nd May, however, he attended the opening of the Royal College of Music at South Kensington and the court dress he wore proved no protection against the rigours of an English spring.

He caught a chill and had to take to his bed, and on June 14th he was dead.

Every honour was done to his remains, and a memorial service at Westminster Abbey testified to the great esteem in which he was held, but it was in his own Devon parish that he was buried, his grave being next to that of his first wife. He was seventy-four at the time of his death, twelve years less than the span his father had attained.

CHAPTER VII

Lord Russell of Killowen

Quite an imposing list could be made of solicitors who abandoned that profession, qualified as barristers, and rose to be great judges, and in such a list the name of Lord Russell of Killowen would have a very prominent position. Had it not been for the advice of two well-wishers he would have remained a Belfast solicitor to the end of his life, and although with his powerful personality he could not have failed to make his name, yet he would never have achieved a tithe of the success which he gained in England during a strenuous career extending over forty-two years.

Charles Russell was born in County Down, Ireland, on November 10th, 1832, and, after the usual schooling, expressed a desire to become a solicitor. The Bar was first thought of, but it offered such a poor chance for a young man with no private means that the safer, if more obscure, profession was adopted, and in 1854 Russell was admitted a solicitor. He began to practise in Belfast, and very soon his services were in constant demand.

Even in those days the young solicitor had a strong personality, a resourceful tongue, and an ability to take charge of a case and dominate it. Magistrates never forgot Charles Russell when once he had argued a case before them, and his oratorical efforts met with so much success that he was very quickly amongst the leading practitioners in the Irish city.

But if Russell was by profession a solicitor his mode of conducting a case was that of the barrister, and a County Court judge, before whom he appeared, strongly advised him to study for the Bar, get called in England, and leave the rest to his own talents.

It was, of course, something of a risk, and Russell realised it. As a solicitor he was steadily forging ahead, and a prosperous and happy future seemed assured for him in Ireland. Furthermore, he was engaged to a charming girl, Ellen Mulholland, and young men when they wish to marry think first of a regular income. Still, Russell at heart longed for the bigger scope the English Bar would afford him.

He was, it must be said, of a dominating—his opponents called it domineering—manner. Endowed physically with great strength, possessing a strong, handsome face, and equipped perfectly with all the arts that go towards the formation of a great advocate, the Bar was Russell's natural vocation. He, therefore, retired from the "junior branch" of the law, entered Trinity College, Dublin—because attendance there would shorten his period of probation at the Inns of Court in London—and, of course, he wanted to postpone the hour of parting from his family and Miss Mulholland as long as possible. At the end of two years he came to London to pass his examination.

Two very important events occurred in 1858—his call to the Bar in London and his marriage to Miss Mulholland. Both were accomplished on a capital of one thousand pounds, a present from his mother, but it was quite sufficient for Russell, who faced the future with confidence.

Of course, briefs did not come with a rush, but he had not to serve an apprenticeship to despair, as he began his career as a barrister in Liverpool, where there was a large Irish population, and where, thanks to the friendship of a local solicitor, Russell had a fair share of business.

Young barristers do not wake up in the morning and find themselves famous. They must do a certain amount of spade-work, gain confidence in themselves, and, for a time, progress slowly. Then when the great chance comes, if they are equal to it, fame is theirs and the rest is easy.

While briefs were infrequent Russell found his pen a ready helper, and he earned a good deal by contributing to various papers. But his journalism was, after all, only a side issue. The Bar was his vocation, and no one meeting him doubted that he would make good at it.

He was not a man to be forgotten. Half an hour of Charles Russell and you remembered him for the rest of your life. He had strong opinions on every subject under the sun, could not tolerate fools, gladly gave hard knocks and received them in return with equanimity, sang a song with gusto, and was altogether a live personality whom to know well was to like and admire. Somehow he was always bigger than his cases, and even before his name was a household word amongst his friends and rivals at the Bar it was said that he would be a very big man in the profession one of these days.

His first important brief, however, did not provide him with any opportunity to do more than impress several very distinguished Q.C.'s of the day that successors to their huge practices would not be wanting if young Russell was a specimen of the Junior Bar.

The case was the famous Windham Lunacy Inquiry, conducted by Mr. Samuel Warren, known to fame as the author of "Ten Thousand a Year." It was an extraordinary affair altogether, and it was investigated by the authorities at the request of the youth's uncle, General Windham, who wished to prevent his nephew ruining his life.

William Frederick Windham came of age in August, 1861, inheriting a very fine estate. He was "a bit of an ass," and had the reputation of being eccentric, but when his eccentricity took the form of marrying a girl of dreadful character, whom he had picked out of the street, and when he insisted upon settling huge sums upon her, it was thought desirable that some attempt should be made to curb his activities. A fine property was going to ruin, and a weak-minded young man was destroying himself. Could he be saved from his own follies?

The inquiry lasted for over a month, and Russell was asked to watch it on behalf of the youth's mother, Lady Sophia. Sir Hugh Cairns (afterwards Lord Chancellor), Mr. Karslake, Q.C. (later Attorney-General), and Mr. Milward appeared for Windham, with several other distinguished counsel.

Russell made a speech on behalf of Lady Sophia, explaining her attitude towards the inquiry, which was that of a mother only anxious that the best should be done for her son. It was a fine speech, delivered with great confidence, and it impressed all who heard it. Russell certainly had the great advantage of a "presence," and it did not worry him that amongst his audience were many of the leading barristers in the country. The result of the inquiry was a foolish judgment declaring young Windham to be quite capable of looking after his own affairs.

By now Russell was making over a thousand a year, and his name was established amongst his contemporaries on the northern circuit. There was no longer any need for him to invite briefs. They came in a flood, and with each year his income increased notably. Naturally he did not attain success without paying a price, and his brusque manner irritated many. Pompous solicitors who considered that they ought to be treated with great deference by the barristers they believed they had "made" were startled and annoyed by Russell's attitude towards them.

Once a person of this type, enveloped in a huge fur coat, came to see the Irish barrister about a certain case in which he had briefed him. Russell was very busy, and the sight of the over-fed and overdressed lawyer annoyed him.

"Sit down," he said, curtly, nodding towards a chair. "I'll talk to you presently."

Half an hour later the visitor began to shuffle in his chair.

"Don't do that," snapped the barrister. "I can't bear a noise."

The solicitor's body became rigid, but after another interval he ventured to draw attention to his presence.

Russell flung aside a brief and rose.

"What are you here for?" he asked, taking a delight in tormenting the man, whom he knew had a great opinion of himself, and to whom most of the Junior Bar kow-towed.

The lawyer explained his business.

"Ah, yes, I understand," said Russell, quietly. "I don't think I'll detain you. There's nothing fresh you can tell me. Good morning."

The offended visitor hastened to leave the room, vowing to himself that he would never give another brief to Charles Russell, but half-way down the stairs a stentorian voice bellowed a command for him to return.

"He wishes to apologise," said the solicitor, recovering a little. "I suppose it's his Irish humour."

When he reached the landing outside the door the now busy barrister called out again—"You forgot to close the door, Mr. Blank, and I hate draughts."

It was characteristic of Russell. If he liked a man he would do anything for him, but once he came to the conclusion that an acquaintance was a fool or a prig he treated him mercilessly. He worked at everything, even his recreations. He loved racing and card-playing, but he was a trying partner at the latter. It was always a case of wherever Russell sat was the head of the table. His strong, forceful personality would insist upon dominating everybody. Still, he did not always have his own way.

There is a good story told of him when he was Lord Chief Justice. One evening he dropped in at one of his clubs for a game of whist, or it may have been bridge, which he was just in time to learn before he died. Three others were found to make a table, and Russell took his seat, as usual, with a certain dignity that solemnised the proceedings. The players "cut," and Russell's partner was a young guardsman rejoicing in his new commission and budding moustache. Probably he was a good soldier, but as a card-player he was impossible. The play began, and soon Lord Russell was fuming, finally bursting into a torrent of angry expostulations. The guardsman waited until the eloquence had ceased. Then, in the coolest manner possible, he leaned over the table, and very incisively said—" Look here, Russell, you're not in your wretched little police court now, so you mustn't talk to me like that."

Only those who knew Russell and his opinion of the great position he held can appreciate his speechless horror at the term " wretched little police court " applied to the scene of his judicial activities.

It is impossible, of course, to even mention the cases in which he appeared during his thirty-six years at the Bar, and a selection must be made. I will not give them in order of date.

One of the most remarkable, Nuttall *v.* Wildes, for breach of promise of marriage, is now forgotten, but it deserves to be recorded.

Captain Wildes divorced his wife, and after a short interval met a Miss Nuttall, and proposed to her. The girl accepted him, and preparations were hurried forward for the marriage, and it was in connection with these preparations that Captain Wildes paid a visit to London. He was walking down Regent Street, when he saw a lady approaching him whose face and figure seemed familiar. As she came nearer, the captain thought he had not seen a more attractive lady, and when she had gone past him he turned to have another look at her. Simultaneously the lady turned to glance at him, and in that moment the short-sighted officer recognised his divorced wife! Something impelled him to go up to her, and five minutes later they were seated in a tea-shop talking over old times.

Captain Wildes discovered that he had been a little unjust to her, but, far more important than that, he realised that he still loved his wife and the mother of his children, and that she was the only woman in the world for him. Thereupon he asked her to make it up again, and, having obtained her consent, he married her again within a week.

Charles Russell was seen at his best when he came to address the jury on behalf of Captain Wildes. It was a case which appealed strongly to him, for with all his apparent brusqueness he was sentimental at heart. Russell was in his element, and although the jury awarded three thousand pounds damages to Miss Nuttall it was felt that counsel for the defendant had scored a success. His speech was a masterpiece of eloquence and reasoning, and it did a lot towards acquainting the greater public with the remarkable gifts of the brilliant Irishman.

Another brief he held was for the defendant in the celebrated case, Belt *v.* Lawes, a trial which lasted forty-three days, and one which excited fierce controversies and parted many friends. When Russell was retained for the defendant he must have anticipated an easy victory, but once again he lost because facts were too strong for him.

Richard Belt was a sculptor, who had gained a good position in the art world. Upon hearing rumours charging him with fraudulently passing off certain busts and statues as his own work when they were clearly the productions of others, he brought an action for libel against his traducer, Mr. Lawes, also a sculptor, and, after forty-three days, got a verdict of five thousand pounds in his favour.

Perhaps there never was so much contradictory evidence given by experts as in this trial. The famous artists, Leighton and Millais, were witnesses for Mr. Lawes, who had practically all the members of the Royal Academy to back him up, and they contested Belt's right to call himself a sculptor. But a supreme test was ordered, and it really decided the case. Belt was asked to do a bust while the trial was in progress, and a place was set apart for him, and as he worked members of the jury came in and watched him.

When the bust was finished and compared with the one he had been told to copy, Leighton and Millais said there was no artistic merit in the copy, and that the original was a fine piece of work, quite beyond the ability of the plaintiff. And yet Mr. Belt brought forward witnesses who swore that they had seen him make the original bust!

Russell had a hard task, but for a long time it appeared certain that he would gain the verdict. He had the most reputable witnesses, and almost every art expert was on his side.

But Mr. Belt fought tenaciously, and there was a lot of sympathy for him; indeed, his costly defence was paid for by the subscriptions of thousands of persons, most of whom had never seen him. But they were sorry for a self-made man whose career was in danger of being ruined by what they called the "jealousy of the Academicians."

A brilliant speech from Russell did not prevent the jury returning a verdict for the plaintiff, and, as I have said, he was awarded five thousand pounds damages.

When the defendant asked for a new trial it was refused. However, the damages were never paid, as Mr. Lawes went bankrupt purposely to avoid paying them.

A little over three years elapsed and once again Russell opposed Mr. Belt, but this time it was a criminal trial, and the sculptor was faced with a charge of having obtained several thousand pounds from Sir William Abdy by fraud.

A change had taken place in Russell's fortunes, too. He was now Sir Charles Russell, Q.C., M.P. (for Hackney), and Her Majesty's Attorney-General. He led the prosecution, and Belt was convicted and sentenced to twelve months' imprisonment, with hard labour.

I can only name a few of his most important cases before I proceed to deal with him as a judge. He acted for Lady Colin Campbell in the Campbell divorce suit, a *cause célèbre* which divided society and led to some of the most remarkable revelations a court of law has ever had to listen to. Both petitions were dismissed—a victory for Russell.

He represented the Irish Party at the Parnell Commission, and gained a great personal triumph, his final speech being one of the finest ever delivered by counsel, while his cross-examination of Pigott, the forger, was magnificent. Pigott was so lacerated by the cross-examination that he fled from England and committed suicide rather than go into the witness-box and face Sir Charles Russell again.

Mary Ann Cotton, the poisoner, was prosecuted by Russell, and if ever a woman merited death it was this vile creature, who murdered her relatives and friends without the slightest compunction. Certainly, Russell saw to it that she had no chance of escaping just punishment.

In cases where he believed in the guilt of the prisoner he was merciless, and allowed no sentiment to sway him.

The time came when Russell was bound to accept a judgeship, and had he not been a Roman Catholic he would have been appointed Lord

Chancellor by Mr. Gladstone, but that was out of the question, and in 1894 he became a Lord of Appeal, and was created a life peer under the title of Lord Russell of Killowen.

He had certainly earned the comparative repose of the Bench, and it was expected that he would make a great judge. These expectations he realised, although the "old Adam" was always there, and the quick temper and brusque manner sometimes startled his court and alarmed counsel. Shortly after his appointment to the House of Lords the Lord Chief Justice, Coleridge, died, and Russell succeeded him, and in the six years he occupied the post he gained the reputation of being one of the best chiefs in the long history of that illustrious office.

As Lord Chief Justice his most notable trial was that of the Jameson Raiders in 1896. He had two other judges to assist him, but from the beginning he took the case in hand, and it was all Russell and no one else. The prisoners were, of course, immensely popular and extremely influential, and it was generally expected that they would be acquitted amid acclamation, but the Lord Chief Justice knew that the raiders had been guilty of an offence against a friendly nation.

The South African Republics had their rights and no English court of law could encourage lawless raids, however well meant, by subjects of Queen Victoria. The Chief was anxious that neither patriotism nor partisanship should tarnish the reputation British justice has, but when, by carefully steering the jury, he had gained his object—a verdict of guilty—he inflicted only nominal sentences, and even these were not served in full.

However, Lord Russell had vindicated the character of the law, for he did not wish the world to think that Englishmen were encouraged to violate the territory of friendly nations.

The greatest service Russell rendered this country was his work as an arbitrator on behalf of Great Britain in the Venezuelan boundary dispute. This was an affair which at one time appeared certain to lead to war between Britain and the United States.

For many years Venezuela had disputed Britain's claim to certain land adjoining British Guiana, and the United States, wishing to end the matter, suggested arbitration. This was rejected by Lord Salisbury, then Prime Minister, and when his decision was notified the American President decided to appoint a special commission to settle the matter irrespective of Britain's wishes.

Of course, Britain could not accept such a high-handed proceeding, and the controversialists on both sides raised their voices and shrieked defiance at one another. But eventually we agreed to arbitration, and Lord Russell was appointed with Lord Justice Collins to represent Great Britain.

Russell was chief arbitrator, and the case was one which eminently called for the exercise of those masterful qualities which had been the terror of many a judge when he was at the Bar. But at the same time he never forgot that justice must be done, and when the final award was made it was found that he had preserved Britain's interests without violating the rights of the weak. Each side got something it claimed, but Britain was substantially the gainer.

There is no doubt that Russell was proud of his position as Lord Chief Justice, and that he would not tolerate anything which tended to endanger his dignity.

Like all strong men he was at heart a partisan, and the principal complaint against him was that as soon as he had got the bearings of a case which he was trying he quickly made up his mind, and from that moment until the end was clearly on one side or the other. But this has been said of nearly all strong judges, and in the interests of justice it is only fair that the wisdom and experience of the presiding judge should be cast into the scale on the side of right.

It was, however, amusing to watch Lord Chief Justice Russell rebuking counsel for offences which he himself had been fond of committing. He was always master in his own court, but there were barristers of the first rank who insisted upon conducting their cases as they thought fit, and resenting the Chief's "interference," as they called it. Then there would ensue a brief "scene," but Russell always had the last word. Still, it is on record that the late Sir C. F. Gill, K.C., earned fame by standing up to the redoubtable judge.

In the circumstances it is not to be wondered at that Russell was not a judicial humorist. He had no desire to see his audience rock with laughter at a sally, although he is credited with a few witticisms which are very good. The best is his answer to a question from a distinguished counsel who asked what the heaviest penalty for bigamy was.

"Two mothers-in-law," said Russell promptly.

On another occasion he was listening patiently to a long-winded address which an excited prisoner was delivering, the purport of his remarks being to prove that he was an injured innocent. Lord Russell gave him every attention, but happening not to catch the last few words he said, "What was your last sentence?"

"Six months' hard, my lord," was the unexpected reply.

All great men are human, and have their little weaknesses, and off the Bench Lord Russell was a delightful companion to his intimates. He was very fond of children, and he was one of the best known of the large army of racegoers.

On one occasion he was walking in the vicinity of Newmarket Heath, when he was angrily told to clear off by a suspicious trainer, who openly accused him of being a newspaper tout, but a few well-chosen, sledge-hammer sentences sent the trainer hurrying back to his stables, and Russell proceeded on his way.

Russell was destined to be a judge for six years only. It had been thought that the change from strenuous advocacy to dignified ease on the Bench would prolong his life beyond the allotted three score years and ten, but, although he worked right up to the end, when he reached the middle sixties he must have realised that he was not to attain a green old age.

In 1900, after doing the Welsh circuit, he was seized with illness on his return to London, and an operation was immediately performed by Mr. (now Sir Frederick) Treves.

The operation was successful, but the Chief had not the reserve of strength to keep him going during the necessarily trying period following it, and he passed away shortly afterwards in his sixty-eighth year. He had been Lord Chief Justice for only a little more than six years, but long enough to make his tenure of the post famous and memorable.

CHAPTER VIII

Lord Alverstone

Sheer hard work was mainly responsible for the success of Richard Webster, both as barrister and as Lord Chief Justice of England. He never went into court without having first mastered his brief, and he was one of the few counsel of his day who believed that the best time for study was the morning and not the night. A noted athlete at Charterhouse and Cambridge, he always kept himself in perfect physical condition, and plenty of exercise and early rising were his sovereign remedies for the ills the flesh is heir to. Webster was of medium height, with an impressive cast of features, a kindly disposition, though stern and inflexible when the occasion demanded, and he crowned his great career at the Bar by making an ideal Lord Chief Justice. In private life he was a devout churchman, a devoted parent, and interested in athletics, glee singing, choirs, missionaries, and tracts.

I remember calling upon him a few years after his appointment to the Chief Justiceship. He was due to preside over a sensational murder trial at the Old Bailey, and, of course, while we could not discuss that particular case, I thought I should find him engaged upon the preliminary details, but instead I happened to interrupt him as he was making notes for a speech to be delivered at the annual meeting of the Religious Tract Society.

The learning, conscientiousness, dignity, and sincerity he brought to bear upon his high office were not confined to his official duties, and it can be said of Lord Alverstone that nothing he undertook was too trivial for him to deem unworthy of his best efforts.

Richard Webster, the son of Thomas Webster, Q.C., was born in 1842, and called to the Bar at the age of twenty-six. Ten years later he became Queen's Counsel, the Lord Chancellor bestowing a silk gown on the young man who had one of the largest practices in the courts. He was generally employed by the railway companies, and in patent cases, assessment appeals, arbitrations, and shipping disputes he was often to be found. Very few of his briefs were of public interest, but they brought him a fortune, and the successful barrister had no personal desire to figure in trials which absorbed the attention of the man in the street.

Now and then one of his cases attracted universal notice, but for many years Webster, though a leading counsel, was not as well known outside the law courts as many men his admitted inferiors.

In 1879 the Tay bridge collapsed as a train was passing over it, with the result that more than eighty lives were lost. An inquiry was held by the railway commissioners, and Webster appeared for the contractors. Faulty construction was, of course, the cause of that terrible accident in the darkness of a late December night, and the engineer responsible—Sir William Bouch—died shortly after giving evidence at the inquiry, owing to the shock the tragic affair had caused him. This was one of the first sensational cases with which Webster was associated, but it eventually proved to be only one of very many.

In the year 1881 a railway porter, Thomas, who lived at Leominster, lost by death his only lodger, an elderly man of the name of Whalley. In the neighbourhood it had been rumoured that Whalley was well off, but everybody was surprised to hear that he had left behind him the large fortune of one hundred thousand pounds. When a will was found it was seen that except for two legacies, one of five thousand pounds to Whalley's nephew—really his illegitimate son—and one of one hundred pounds to a local friend, the whole of the estate was left to Thomas.

Now Whalley had never been married, but he had two children, a boy and a girl, who were called his nephew and niece, and to whom he was attached. They instantly expressed doubts as to the authenticity of the Thomas will, and an action was entered, the nephew—as I will continue to call him—retaining Sir Charles Russell and the next-of-kin obtaining the services of Webster.

The nephew swore that his uncle had made a will bequeathing the property to himself and his sister, but as this will could not be produced, and the signature to that presented for probate by Thomas was undoubtedly genuine, all the parties concerned agreed to a compromise. The estate was divided into three parts—one each for the nephew, the next-of-kin, and Thomas—each share amounting to over thirty thousand pounds.

The nephew was so pleased with the result that he organised a sort of demonstration, driving round Leominster in a brake with a man blowing a bugle. As he was passing the cottage where Thomas lived, the latter waved a piece of blue foolscap paper at him. Instantly the nephew remembered that the will in his favour had been written on similar paper, and he told his solicitor, adding that he believed Thomas had it in his possession.

Inquiries were set on foot, and certain extraordinary facts were discovered. It appeared that shortly before his death Whalley had dictated a letter to Thomas, in which he asked his nephew to call and see him at once. Thomas had taken down the old man's words in pencil, but had asked Whalley to sign the letter in ink so that the nephew might be convinced that it was genuine. Accordingly, Whalley had written his signature, and then Thomas had called in the aid of a solicitor's clerk, who had erased the pencil writing and had inserted a "last will and testament," which made Thomas a rich man.

There were two more trials subsequently, the first one taking place in a civil court, when Webster obtained an order setting aside the compromise originally arrived at. The new judgment gave two-thirds of the hundred thousand pounds to the nephew and the balance to the next-of-kin. The last trial was in a criminal court, when the conspirators were sentenced for fraud and forgery.

It is interesting to note that had not Thomas been so foolish as to wave the piece of blue foolscap at the nephew, the latter would never have attempted to probe further into the matter, and, instead of finding his way into a convict's cell, the railway porter would have been a rich man for the rest of his days.

In 1885 Webster was returned to the House of Commons as member for Launceston, appointed

Attorney-General, and knighted. It was a wonderful tribute to his success that he should become head of the Bar without having to serve as Solicitor-General.

Webster was by now, of course, a prominent public figure. He had a personality outside the law as well as in it, and his early rising habits and his membership of the choir of Kensington parish church gave rise to several stories. It was said that he usually fixed six o'clock in the morning for consultations with his juniors, and that one nervous young barrister—now a judge, by the way—was so anxious not to be late for the appointment with his chief that he sat up all night to keep it.

Another story concerned a convivial member of the Bar, who was retained to act with Webster in an important civil suit. Webster sent a note asking his "learned friend" to call at his chambers at six the following morning. The convivial one stared hard at it for several minutes. Then he seized a pen and wrote the following answer :—

"Dear Webster,—Sorry I cannot keep the appointment. It is much too late for me, as I like to be in bed not later than four."

Whether the story is true or not, it illustrates the mild sensation caused by the thorough-going and almost revolutionary methods of "Dicky" Webster.

As Attorney-General, Sir Richard Webster could no longer avoid criminal work, and he was engaged in many important cases. When in 1887 John Burns and Cunninghame Graham caused a riot in Trafalgar Square—how long ago it seems now !—he prosecuted on behalf of the Government, and the accused were sentenced to terms of imprisonment.

After comparatively mild offenders such as

these agitators were, there was much more exciting work in bringing about the punishment of dangerous anarchists and ruffians who did not hesitate to murder inoffensive citizens. Along with all concerned in these trials, Webster was plagued with anonymous letters threatening him with a terrible death, but, of course, he was quite unaffected by methods so characteristic of bullies and cowards.

Jabez Balfour was another celebrated criminal who was prosecuted by Webster, and although the case was protracted and complicated it cannot be denied that the task of the prosecution in securing a conviction was an easy one. Balfour was sent to penal servitude for fourteen years, and, after serving his sentence and enjoying several years of liberty, died a short time ago at the age of seventy-one. As Attorney-General Webster led for the Crown at the trial of the Jameson Raiders, and he appeared for *The Times* before the Parnell Commission. He also represented Great Britain before the arbitrators who decided the Venezuelan boundaries and the Behring Sea disputes.

Before I pass on to Sir Richard Webster's elevation to the Bench I must refer to a case in which he was concerned which had an amusing side to it. In 1891 a girl of the name of Daisy Hopkins committed the " crime " of walking in the streets of Cambridge with an undergraduate.

This was an offence against the University statutes, and Daisy was promptly carried off to the University prison, known as the Spinning House. Here she was kept incarcerated whilst her friends applied to the courts for her release, and this was eventually granted, despite the arguments of Webster, who maintained that the law was on the side of the dons. However, the girl had to be set free, and she retaliated by bringing an action for false imprisonment against the University of Cambridge, but she lost her case, the jury—it was tried at Ipswich—holding that residents in the town were bound to observe the rules of the University.

A few months before the death of Lord Chief Justice Russell, Webster was induced to accept the position of Master of the Rolls. He had refused it some years earlier, but it happened that Lord Russell's death give him the position he coveted, and in 1900 he became Lord Chief Justice. It was generally agreed that he was the best man to follow Russell, and during the thirteen years he was on the Bench he proved that he was at least as competent as his great predecessor.

The Yarmouth Beach murder is still remembered, principally because of the magnificent efforts of Mr. Marshall Hall, K.C., to secure the acquittal of his client, Herbert John Bennett. Bennett was a married man, with one daughter, and he seems to have grown tired of his wife even before he met the girl whom he wished to marry and whom he succeeded in convincing that he was a single man. Mrs. Bennett was staying at Yarmouth in September, 1900, and occasionally her husband visited her, though he always came reluctantly. He grudged having to give her money, and, indeed, from the time the other girl came into his life he brooded on the inconvenience of having a wife as an obstacle to his desires. On the 22nd day of that month he went down to Yarmouth and met Mrs. Bennett.

Late that night they went down to the beach, and appeared to have been there quite alone and unobserved for at least half an hour. What took place before the murder we shall never know, but Bennett undoubtedly left for London by a late train, and a few hours after his departure the body of his wife was discovered on the beach. She had been strangled with a boot-lace.

It was a weird, haunting sort of tragedy that immediately gripped the imagination of the public, and when Bennett was arrested popular excitement was tremendous. Everything depended upon the ability of the prosecution to prove that Bennett had a motive for wishing to murder his wife, and also that he had been in Yarmouth on that fatal Saturday. With Mr. Marshall Hall to defend him he had, of course, the best ability at the Bar, and the fact that the Lord Chief Justice of England presided emphasised the great importance of the case.

Both sides fought the contest with all the resources at their command. Lord Alverstone watched over the proceedings with his usual dignity and wisdom. Never an interfering judge, he always knew when to step in, and probably no Chief Justice had fewer "scenes" in his court than he had.

As all the world knows, Mr. Marshall Hall's efforts were in vain, and Bennett was rightly convicted and executed. The prosecution proved that he could have been nowhere else but at Yarmouth at the time of the murder, and, as there was no doubt as to the motive for the crime, the jury returned a verdict against the accused.

A rather remarkable case marked the closing months of the South African War. Dr. Krause, a Boer, had been removed to England as a prisoner of war, and when under restraint had written letters inciting certain persons to murder

Mr. Foster, who was also a citizen of the Transvaal Republic. Mr. Rufus Isaacs, as he then was—he is now Lord Reading and Viceroy of India—defended Krause, who was found guilty and sentenced by Lord Alverstone to two years' imprisonment with hard labour.

When Roger Casement was tried for high treason seven years ago the only modern precedents for such a case were found in the records of the trial of Arthur Lynch before Lord Alverstone and two other judges in 1903. Lynch, although a British subject, had fought for the Boers against Britain, but, knowing that there was little likelihood of his being executed for his crime, he had returned to Ireland. He was arrested and arraigned at the Old Bailey, and, as it could not be disputed that he had been guilty of the offence with which he was charged, he was sentenced to death, a sentence which there was no intention of carrying out. However, Lynch was kept in prison for about eighteen months and then released. Later on a full pardon enabled him to enter the House of Commons and as such draw a salary of four hundred pounds a year from the British taxpayers.

It is instructive to remember this, as there is not another country in the world where a man could be convicted of such a serious crime and shortly afterwards allowed to take part in making the laws for the country whose enemies he had assisted.

The story of the murder of Mr. Whiteley, "the Universal Provider," as he loved to style himself, is one of the most dramatic in the records of crime. Everybody knew Whiteley, and in his old age he was remarkable for his benevolent appearance and his fondness for quoting Scripture.

He had become a millionaire entirely owing to his ability and enterprise, and he was one of the most vivid personalities in London business circles. A vast army of employees owed him allegiance, and he had the reputation of being a generous and good-natured master.

I remember an interview with Whiteley a few days before his death. He talked at length on modern ways of stimulating business, and, while criticising the introduction of American methods, he did not fail to see and to admit that there was something attractive about them. That he lived for the great business he had built up was very evident. Nothing else was of real importance to him. The rest of the world seemed made to serve the interests of his emporium.

Once he called upon Frith, the painter of "Derby Day" and other gigantic canvases, and offered him a huge fee if he would paint a picture of Whiteley's, showing it at its busiest. Frith declined, greatly to the mystification of the "Universal Provider," who could not understand where the "loss of dignity" came in. Perhaps Whiteley was before his time.

Rayner, the murderer, was apparently a highly-strung person, with what some people call the artistic temperament. That is, he did not like work, and, as he had plenty of time to waste, he wasted it brooding over a grievance which he alleged he had with William Whiteley. Some one had told him a romantic story of a beautiful girl who had been promised marriage by the then struggling tradesman, how the girl had been betrayed and deserted, and so on. The story had nothing novel about it, but Rayner worked himself up into a passion about it, hinted that he ought to be rich beyond the dreams of avarice, and one morning walked into Mr. Whiteley's office at Westbourne Grove, revolver in hand, and shot the old man dead.

He was easily captured, and soon found his way to the Old Bailey. The vast majority of murderers are convicted on circumstantial evidence, but in Rayner's case there were several eye-witnesses of the deed, and, however sensational the crime and no matter how feverishly excited the public were, it had necessarily to be a short trial.

Lord Alverstone presided, and, although a vast amount of irrelevant matter was introduced, the plain fact was proved that Rayner had murdered Whiteley. He was convicted and sentenced to death, but the world continued to talk of the grim tragedy. Rumour manufactured romances by the score, and every gossip in the country pretended to have discovered a hitherto unknown cause for the drama. Mr. Herbert Gladstone was then Home Secretary, and he gave the finishing touch to a sensational affair by reprieving Rayner. Everybody was amazed, with the possible exception of Mr. Gladstone. Even Lord Alverstone, who presumably had all sources of information at his disposal, has recorded his own astonishment, but there was nothing to be done.

Rayner, however, soon rebelled against prison life, and tried to put an end to it by self-starvation. Perhaps he may have thought that if he fasted long enough he would be released. But they deal thoroughly with murderers, and Rayner, for all his bravado, had not the strength of mind that distinguished many weak women in the far-off days of militant suffragettism.

One of his hunger strikes ended abruptly at the sight of a juicy beef-steak, which he seized and devoured, and another was terminated by forcible feeding, and there his efforts ceased. But there are numerous prison warders to-day who wish that Mr. Gladstone had not advised his Majesty to spare the life of the cold-blooded murderer, who was released on medical grounds in March, 1919.

Besides criminal trials Lord Alverstone took part in the final hearing in the House of Lords of the dispute between the United Presbyterian Church of Scotland and the Free Church. He was one of the majority which decided in favour of the Free Church, and gave the latter body more money than it could do with, but a special commission subsequently adjusted matters between the disputants, and a costly and protracted litigation came to an end.

Motiveless crimes are fairly common, but one of the most difficult to understand was the murder of Sir Curzon Wyllie by a Hindoo about twelve years ago. Dhingra, an unpleasant type of native, who lost any remnant of civilisation he may have possessed from the day he began to be educated on European lines, was a law student in London. The India Office has a special department which looks after the interests of students from our Eastern Empire, and Sir Curzon Wyllie, an Indian administrator of great experience, was one of the best friends native Indians had in London.

It was inexplicable that Dhingra should have selected him to be his victim, yet when Sir Curzon attended a reception at the Imperial Institute, Dhingra went to it with the intention of murdering one of the benefactors of his class. The murderer was a weak-looking, narrow-chested youth, and when afterwards questioned as to his motive, he said, with a simper, that he had slain Sir Curzon in order to win notoriety for himself.

Dhingra was tried before Lord Alverstone, and, of course, convicted and sentenced to death. As in the Rayner case, there was the direct evidence of eye-witnesses, and no time had to be spent on arguments about the reliability of circumstantial evidence. After Lord Alverstone had pronounced sentence the convict thanked him, and, with an inscrutable smile, left the dock. Dhingra was a type of criminal which re-appears at intervals, and against whom it is impossible to take precautions, for if a man is willing to sacrifice his own life he can murder whom he pleases. But that the guide, philosopher, and friend of Indians in London should have been the victim in this case was, and still is, amazing.

The Crippen case is too recent to be dealt with at length, but Lord Alverstone, who took a great interest in the affair from the day it was known that human remains had been found in the house in Hilldrop Crescent, Camden Town, went down to the Old Bailey to decide the fate of the "doctor" who had startled the world by the murder of his wife. The dramatic attempt at escape to America—the girl disguised as a boy—reads like a romance, and Chief Inspector Walter Dew's arrest of Crippen on board ship was quite unique.

The late Sir Melville Macnaughton, once Assistant Commissioner at New Scotland Yard, expressed the opinion that Crippen might have escaped had he not taken the girl with him. Her presence drew the curiosity of strangers towards him, and her odd disguise caused both to be closely scrutinised, for Ethel Le Neve was not able to hide her sex by donning male attire. That led to their arrest.

Mr. Tobin, K.C., now a knight and a popular County Court judge, defended Crippen, and the trial extended into the fifth day. Of course, the prosecution relied on circumstantial evidence, and as only part of the remains of the unfortunate woman had been found, identification was not easy. But the question was settled to the satisfaction of the jury when the prosecution produced proof positive that a certain scar on the body had been caused by an operation to which Belle Elmore—Mrs. Crippen's stage name, and by which she was generally referred to at the trial—had submitted a year or so before her strange disappearance.

As is nearly always the case with murderers who display utter callousness in taking human life, Crippen was desperately afraid of death and as a forlorn hope he appealed to the Court of Criminal Appeal. But, of course, he had no chance, and the hangman claimed him for his own in due course.

There have been numerous callous and cold-blooded murderers, but surely Crippen was the worst of all in this respect. He murdered his wife, buried her under the floor of a cellar, and then went on living in the same house, and living luxuriously, too. He gave dinner parties and suppers which were often commented upon in the neighbourhood, and the policeman on point duty often saw him bidding farewell to his guests, apparently the most care-free man in that densely populated London district.

The murder of Nisbet, the colliery cashier, by Dickman formed one of the sensations of the year which also witnessed the trial of Crippen. Mr. Justice Coleridge tried the case, and the convicted prisoner appealed. Lord Alverstone and two other judges formed the Court of Criminal Appeal for the purpose of hearing the arguments of Dickman's counsel, and it was the Lord Chief Justice who delivered judgment confirming the sentence of the court below.

Railway murders are notorious for the absence of direct evidence, though in England not one such trial has resulted in the escape of the accused. This is due to the fact that the authorities have never charged a suspect unless they have had a very strong case against him. Dickman's arrest was followed by a subscription in Newcastle to provide for his defence, and on the day before his execution London was patrolled by sandwichmen with boards calling upon the people to make the Home Secretary grant a reprieve, whilst handbills were distributed and telegrams showered upon the members of the Government.

Why this strong feeling on behalf of the convict was aroused one cannot say. Perhaps there is a large body of opinion in Great Britain opposed to conviction in capital trials on circumstantial evidence. However, Dickman was executed, and there could have been no other sequel to a very brutal crime.

After holding office for thirteen years, Lord Alverstone retired, and for two more years battled with ill-health, but in December, 1915, he succumbed at the age of seventy-three. His title died with him, his only son having predeceased him, but his name will endure in the legal history of his country.

In conclusion I will give an anecdote which he keenly relished himself. One Sunday morning an American lady entered Kensington Parish Church bent upon seeing the then Attorney-General in the choir. As a preliminary she drew the verger aside and whisperingly asked him to point out the great man, but the church official was unimpressed.

"You see, ma'am," he said, "there's me and the vicar, but as for the choir, well, as long as they behaves themselves we make no inquiries as to their antecedents."

CHAPTER IX

Lord Chief Justice Cockburn

As his name implies, Cockburn came of a distinguished Scottish family. His father was a well-to-do diplomat and his mother was of French extraction. He was carefully educated, winding up at Trinity Hall, Cambridge, where he took honours in English and Latin, and when twenty-seven years of age he was called to the Bar.

Cockburn was a man of small stature, with plain features, but he had a personality which carried all before it. No one could resist his melodious voice, his ready wit, and his undeviating courtesy. He was a companion in whose society it was impossible to feel depressed, for Cockburn all through the seventy-eight years of his life lived every moment.

When he became a barrister, and was waiting for briefs, he did not pine in gloomy chambers or sit moodily amongst the unbriefed at the back of a court. Instead he plunged into the gaieties that London afforded, attended supper parties, made the acquaintance of the leading actors and actresses of the day, patronised the sporting fraternity, and was a well-known figure at Rosherville and Vauxhall Gardens when the respectability of these Victorian places of amusement was in doubt.

He was very human, but if he rubbed shoulders with the underworld he never became contaminated. Had he done so, he would never have become Lord Chief Justice of England, because he was too strong a man not to make enemies, and, while always profoundly courteous, especially to the weaker sex, he never failed to hit back when attacked.

When he was an old man and Lord Chief Justice an attempt was made during the progress of a great trial—that of Arthur Orton, for perjury—to rake up the past and cast odium upon his character because of alleged wildness in the days of his youth. The attack failed, however. The administration of justice did not suffer in Cockburn's hands because he had not dwelt in priggish seclusion when he was unknown to fame. A judge is none the worse for knowing something of the world.

Some years of steady work enabled Cockburn to win the plaudits of his colleagues at the Bar. Whilst listening to the musical eloquence of the under-sized Scotsman they forgot his physical insignificance, and only saw the great orator and brilliant advocate. It was the same in the drawing-rooms of Mayfair. Young ladies would turn away from the young lawyer, repelled by his unimportance amid a company which included plenty of the "Johnnies" of the day, but within half an hour, when Cockburn had had time to say a few words here and there to friends, he would have every lady in the room hungry for a *tête-à-tête* with him. The magnetism of the man was irresistible.

The first celebrated case with which his name was coupled as one of the chief counsel engaged was the trial in 1843 of MacNaghten for the murder of Mr. Drummond, the private secretary to Sir Robert Peel.

The affair was a most peculiar one.

MacNaghten, a Scotsman, got the idea that Sir Robert Peel was a danger to the nation and that if he were removed it would mean the salvation of the country. Accordingly he decided to be the instrument by which Britain was to be saved, and he went to the neighbourhood of the Houses of Parliament with the intention of waiting for Sir Robert and shooting him on sight. As he was waiting and watching, a gentleman came down Parliament Street, having obviously just left the House of Commons. The fanatical Scotsman instantly came to the conclusion that this was Sir Robert Peel, and thereupon he shot him. Mr. Drummond died of the wound, and MacNaghten was arrested.

Cockburn, who had become Q.C. in 1841, was leading counsel for the defence, which was one of insanity, and, as in those days insanity entitled the accused to be acquitted and set at liberty, it meant that no punishment was inflicted if the defence established its plea. Cockburn handled the defence in a fashion that savoured of genius. Popular prejudice was against his client, and certainly poor Drummond, a most inoffensive person, had been murdered for no fault of his own. The public, therefore, demanded that the assassin should be convicted and executed, but Cockburn brought the judge, Chief Justice Tindal, round to his way of thinking, and eventually Sir William Follett, who prosecuted, had to agree to a verdict of acquittal on the ground of insanity. MacNaghten was, therefore, released.

The usual honours came to the now famous barrister. In 1850 he was appointed Solicitor-General, and a year later Attorney-General, being knighted on his first accession to office, and he was more than an ornamental head of the Bar.

The force, genius, and amazing industry of the man were admitted and admired, and when in 1856 the series of murders committed by Palmer, of Rugeley, excited and horrified the country, Sir Alexander Cockburn was selected to prosecute him at the Central Criminal Court. The trial had been removed from Rugeley because of the strong local prejudice against Palmer.

In connection with this a good story is told of Lord Palmerston, then Prime Minister. A deputation from Rugeley waited upon him in Downing Street to ask for official approval for the changing of the name of Rugeley, which had become notorious through the misdeeds of the poisoner. The locals wished to have a new name, but it was necessary to obtain Government sanction.

"Very well, gentlemen," said "Pam," with quiet sarcasm, "do as you like, but why not honour me by giving your charming town my name?"

Nothing more was heard of the matter after that.

Cockburn's performance in the Palmer trial was considered to be his supreme achievement at the Bar. The talented legal team which was defending the poisoner endeavoured to confuse the issue and puzzle the jury by bringing in medical and legal subtleties, but Cockburn soon demolished the structure the defence raised. He pointed out that murder had been done, and that the murderer must be punished, and he proceeded to prove that Palmer was the guilty one.

Palmer was absorbed by the speech. Throughout the whole of it he kept his eyes on the great lawyer, fascinated in the way that a rabbit is by the approach of the snake's deadly jaw.

The poisoner, a devotee of the turf, described Cockburn's speech in a significant sentence. When the judge had sentenced him to death, Palmer scribbled these words on a piece of paper, "It's the riding that's done it," and sent it to his counsel.

The "riding" was his sporting term for Cockburn's masterly reply for the prosecution.

Before I pass on to Cockburn's promotion to the Bench, I must refer to an interesting will suit in which he was concerned as counsel. Samuel Swynfen died in 1854, leaving to his widowed daughter-in-law, Mrs. Patience Swynfen, sixty thousand pounds. But the testator made no mention of another large estate which he owned, and on his death Mrs. Patience claimed it as well as the property which had been left her. A nephew of Samuel's, however, came forward as another claimant, and finally recourse was had to the law to determine the succession.

Sir F. Thesiger, afterwards Lord Chancellor, was leading counsel for the lady, and Sir Alexander Cockburn looked after the interests of F. H. Swynfen, the nephew of the testator.

Mrs. Swynfen, a woman of rare determination, was ready to spend every penny to enforce her rights, and her astonishment and anger were, therefore, not insignificant when it was announced in court that her counsel had come to an agree ment with the opposite party. She instantly disclaimed all knowledge of the proposed settlement, which she repudiated in the warmest language, charging Sir F. Thesiger with having betrayed her interests, and she applied at once for a new trial. This was granted, and a new personality now appeared in the suit. This was Mr. Charles Kennedy, a barrister, who undertook to see that justice should be done to the lady. She was so captivated by his chivalry and his whole-hearted championship of her cause that she promised to pay him twenty thousand pounds if he succeeded in gaining a verdict for her.

With such a reward in prospect Mr. Kennedy devoted himself entirely to the matter, and during the long litigation he abandoned everything else in order to gain a big estate for Mrs. Swynfen and a fortune for himself, and his efforts—so far as obtaining a favourable verdict was concerned—were successful. Patience Swynfen was declared to be the sole owner of the enormous estate of the late Samuel Swynfen, her father-in-law. Mr. Kennedy congratulated his client and went home, expecting, no doubt, a cheque for twenty thousand pounds in the course of a few days.

The cheque, however, never came, and when he reminded her of her promise she calmly informed him that she had no intention of fulfilling it. She was now Mrs. Broun, having married since the start of the litigation, and once she was in possession of the property it seemed unnecessary to her to part with such a large sum.

Kennedy brought an action to recover, and won, but the Court of Appeal reversed the judgment, and he obtained nothing. Before this the incensed lady had entered an action against her first counsel, Thesiger, known to fame as Lord Chelmsford and Lord High Chancellor, but she was unsuccessful, and the failure of Mr. Kennedy in the Appeal Court to sustain his initial victory ended in 1864 a series of law cases which had begun in the early part of 1856.

Shortly before his elevation to the Bench as

Chief Justice of the Common Pleas Cockburn had an encounter with a policeman in the Haymarket which almost led to his spending the night in a cell. He was walking with Serjeant Ballantine, the celebrated barrister, when he saw a policeman roughly treating a woman. Stopping to remonstrate with the man in blue, the Attorney-General was horrified to find himself gripped by the arm, and curtly informed that he was under arrest for "obstructing the police in the execution of their duty."

With a haughty glare the head of the Bar asked the constable if he knew the person he was addressing.

"Don't know and don't care," was the answer, given in contemptuous tones. "All I know is that you must come along to Vine Street and see the inspector, and your friend must come, too, for trying to rescue you from lawful custody."

Cockburn fixed the fellow with his eye.

"I am Sir Alexander Cockburn, the Attorney-General," he said, in his most impressive manner, "and my friend here is Mr. Serjeant Ballantine."

"Gammon!" retorted the officer, with a glance at the little man. "I've heard that tale before. You've got to come along."

And they went, and found an equally sceptical inspector at the station.

However, at the critical moment a gentleman who knew both of them happened to call to see the inspector, and his identification of the two raging barristers was sufficient to secure for them their release.

When Lord Palmerston, as Foreign Secretary, had been savagely attacked in the House of Commons it was Cockburn, member for Southampton, who had been selected to defend him, and four years later Palmerston was able to reward his brilliant Parliamentary advocate by giving him in 1856 the office of Chief Justice of the Common Pleas, and in 1859 making him Lord Chief Justice.

Cockburn did not trouble to conceal his satisfaction at his elevation. He had had his fill of advocacy, and he wanted a change. From the beginning of his career as a judge he resolved that he would, when possible, try the most remarkable cases himself; and he did not often fail in his ambition. If there was a sensational murder Cockburn arranged his engagements to permit him to preside at the trial of the accused. A will case, or a remarkable libel action, or, indeed, anything which excited the public, was good enough for Sir Alexander.

He selected the actions to be tried by him according to the amount of space they promised to achieve in the newspapers. Of course, now and then he was disappointed. When the Penge Mystery was the one topic throughout the length and breadth of the land the Lord Chief Justice made up his mind that he would take the trial of the Stauntons. It was entered on a special date at the Old Bailey, and Cockburn postponed an important engagement in the provinces in order to be the leading figure in the great drama, but at the last moment he was suddenly called upon in his capacity as Lord Chief Justice to deal with certain very important questions affecting the State, and, to his great sorrow, he had to send Mr. Justice Hawkins to the Old Bailey to try the Stauntons.

Amongst the many claimants now forgotten—the Tichborne impostor threw them all into the shade—the case of Mrs. Ryves deserves a better fate, for this lady made a very daring attempt to prove that she was a legitimate granddaughter of the Duke of Cumberland —George III's brother. It was a remarkable claim, and, as usual, it was founded on a most romantic story.

Mrs. Ryves said that her grandmother, Olive Wilmot, was at the age of seventeen married to Henry Frederick, Duke of Cumberland, and that the issue of the marriage was a daughter, Mrs. Serres, who was her mother.

Numerous documents were introduced into the case, which was heard before Lord Chief Justice Cockburn, Lord Chief Baron Pollock, Sir James Wilde, and a special jury, documents which included alleged marriage certificates, written promises from famous statesmen to see justice done, and correspondence with royal highnesses and others. Mrs. Ryves was anxious to be acclaimed of the blood royal. She wished to shine in society, and, if possible, adopt the title Duchess of Lancaster, which, she said, George III had conferred on her mother, his niece! A document was put in which purported to be a written declaration of the King authorising the issue of the patent.

But the whole case, which seemed in its early stages to foreshadow many sensational revelations of the doings of royalty of an earlier age, weakened considerably when the Attorney-General cross-examined. He proved that the scheme had originated in the brain of Mrs. Serres when that lady was suffering from an imagination which bordered on insanity. The majority of the "proofs" were exposed as forgeries, and Cockburn, in his summing up, described the stories they told as "outrages on all probability."

The verdict of the jury was against Mrs. Ryves, and her curious collection of "proofs" was confiscated by the court, and then the sensation fizzled out.

It had been started several years before by a threat to create a revolution if the claims of the lady were not at once admitted, but the cold atmosphere of a court of justice relegated Mrs. Ryves and her family to that obscure position in society from which they should never have emerged.

It is very seldom that a convict delivers the best speech heard during his trial and moves even his judge to display emotion, but when Cockburn tried Michael Barrett and others for the Clerkenwell explosion of 1867 he had the rare experience of realising that his own admirable charge to the jury and the best efforts of distinguished counsel on both sides were overshadowed by the answer Barrett, who alone was convicted, gave to the usual question as to whether he had anything to say why sentence of death should not be passed upon him. The story of the crime is simple enough.

Two men were imprisoned in the House of Detention to await their trial for treason-felony, and certain of their friends thought they would effect a rescue by placing a barrel of gunpowder against the wall of the prison and exploding it. The plan was carried out, but the prisoners were not rescued, and the result of the crazy crime was that four persons were killed by the explosion and forty injured.

Several arrests were made, and four men and a woman were placed on trial before Cockburn, but Barrett alone was found guilty, and on the clearest evidence. His speech, after conviction, was a remarkable achievement, and the Lord Chief Justice had difficulty in restraining his tears. Two ladies were overcome by emotion, and had to be carried out of court, for the eloquence of the shabby man in the dock profoundly stirred his audience.

He spoke as one standing in the shadow of the gallows, and his eloquence proved that a very successful career would have been his had he not been lured into crime.

The Derby will case was another cause which commanded universal attention. Eight years were spent in the unravelling of the mystery of George Nuttall's will, and it was Lord Chief Justice Cockburn, assisted by a Queen's Bench jury, who eventually solved it.

Nuttall was an uneducated man, who left nearly four thousand a year to his cousin, John Nuttall, a foreman in the employment of a contractor in London. The fortunate heir, however, only lived a year to enjoy his good fortune, and his children naturally expected to inherit their father's wealth. But a fortnight after the death of John Nuttall, a County Court bailiff of Matlock named John Else produced a paper which he swore was a codicil in George Nuttall's handwriting bequeathing to him (Else) his estate. Nine months later he brought forward another codicil in George Nuttall's writing confirming the first, and then clinched the matter with yet a third discovery of a codicil, again in his own favour.

The finding of this last document was remarkable. Else had taken a lease of George Nuttall's old house, and one day he had gone to a hayloft at the back of the yard. He was accompanied by a boy, and Else suddenly came to the conclusion that the window of the loft would be all the better for a thorough cleaning. He thereupon ordered the boy to wash it, but the latter was not tall enough to reach the window-sill, and Else clutched hold of it to pull himself up.

The window-sill, however, must have been in a rotten condition, for it immediately gave way in his hands, disclosing a cavity in the wall in which was an earthenware jar. In the jar was a small bag containing twenty sovereigns, and, astonishing to relate, another codicil, declaring John Else to be George Nuttall's heir! Else hastened to place the remarkable document in the hands of his solicitors, the battle was joined with the family of the late John Nuttall, and the lawyers entered upon their profitable task with zest.

There were four trials, and even the House of Lords was appealed to for a solution of the puzzle. The ablest and most experienced judges sat to hear the arguments for and against.

John Else's remarkable story excited ridicule and disbelief at the first hearing, but he had a considerable amount of fact to support his claim. George Nuttall had been a good business man, but a poor will-maker, and his spelling was unconventional. The Else codicils contained plenty of mistakes in spelling, but they were not the sort of errors that Nuttall had been in the habit of making.

The last trial of all was presided over by Cockburn, who liked this sort of case, because he prided himself upon his knowledge of handwriting and his ability to detect imposture. Three counsel on either side hammered away under the Chief's presidency, and, as usual, there was plenty of perjury and not a few "scenes." Cockburn and his jury, however, settled all doubts by pronouncing against Else, and the great codicil mystery ended.

There was an amusing libel action tried by him

which afforded him the greatest enjoyment. Lieutenant Morrison, the owner of Zadkiel's Almanack, brought an action against Admiral Sir Edward Belcher, who had described the astrologer as a cheat and an impostor. A fashionable gathering assembled in court to see Zadkiel's powers tested. Sir Edward Bulwer Lytton, the novelist, was a believer in astrology, but he denied Morrison's claim to be on familiar terms with the denizens of the spirit world. There was a lot of amusing evidence. The plaintiff was, of course, held up to ridicule, and he lent himself to it by stating that one of his constant visitors when in a supernatural state was St. Luke. A bishop came into court with several other dignitaries of the church to listen to Morrison's account of St. Luke. But the plaintiff was not without his supporters and believers. He had scores of fashionable persons amongst his adherents.

Cockburn enjoyed the case. It gave him numberless opportunities to pass witty remarks, and from beginning to end the court was more like a place of entertainment. Amid the laughter and the jokes the jury heard enough of the arguments to award the redoubtable Zadkiel twenty shillings as adequate damages. The Lord Chief Justice would not, however, grant him his costs, and so both parties, the lieutenant and the admiral, were considerable losers by the litigation.

In the year that witnessed the outbreak of hostilities between France and Prussia, Cockburn presided over a sensational trial for murder, the victim being a clergyman and the murderer a workman.

The Rev. Elias Huelin was elderly and faddy, but a good business man, who developed his estate to the best possible advantage, adding to his income by acting as assistant chaplain to a London cemetery. In order to manage his property he lived in Paulton's Square, Chelsea, where a housekeeper, Ann Boss, formed his sole staff, and attended to his simple requirements. Thousands of persons knew him by sight, but few had the honour of his acquaintance, for he was not addicted to making friends, and this, combined with his well-known habits of frugality, created a general belief that he was very rich.

Amongst the houses owned by Mr. Huelin was No. 25, Wellington Square, Chelsea, and, his tenant's lease having expired, the owner had to redecorate and repair the building with a view to finding another occupant. To this end he engaged a jobbing bricklayer and plasterer to effect the necessary repairs, and the workman —Walter Miller—entered on a job which he was glad to secure; and, as he was cheap, Mr. Huelin thought he had no reason to regret his bargain.

But Walter Miller had a good and sufficient reason for offering himself at a price below the market rate. He was not fond of work, and his usual procedure was to devote a few weeks to honest labour and then proceed to spend his earnings in drink. When penniless and hungry he would seek another job, but deep down in his heart there was always the desire that he would be able to abandon work altogether. He had no clear idea how fortune was to come to him, but, nevertheless, he hoped and he believed that he would not have to work all his life.

The clergyman rather liked him, and Miller certainly could talk intelligently. He worked hard, too, and efficiently, and there was nothing in his demeanour to foreshadow the terrible tragedy.

Mr. Huelin always paid his accounts in person, and generally in cash. He would trust no one, not even his housekeeper, although she was a good and faithful servant to him. Accordingly, at the end of the week, he called at 25, Wellington Square to hand Miller his wages, and while paying him he took a handful of gold coins out of his pocket. The plasterer's eyes glistened when he saw this—to him—evidence of wealth, but he did not betray his sudden greed. His wages were handed to him, and he appeared to be content, but he never forgot the handful of gold, and from that moment his thoughts dwelt on all that such riches would mean to him—no more work and a life of pleasure—the sort of life of which he dreamed.

The following week Mr. Huelin, in paying Miller's wages, again displayed more gold. In the meantime Miller had listened greedily to bar-room stories of the large amount of cash the clergyman kept in his house.

He was aware that Mr. Huelin carried a considerable sum about with him, for the banks did not appear to be popular with the clergyman ; and slowly but surely the fellow convinced himself that here was a chance of making himself rich beyond the dreams of avarice if only he had the necessary courage. Mr. Huelin had no friends apparently who would create trouble if he disappeared. Once the clergyman was out of the way there would only be one other person to silence, and that was the housekeeper, Ann Boss. She could easily be disposed of, and then the hoard of gold at 15, Paulton Square would be his rich reward for the risk.

The temptation was too much for Miller. He lacked just that intelligence which would have pointed out the innumerable difficulties and dangers he would have to encounter when Mr. Huelin's absence was noticed eventually. In a crowded London suburb even the most determined of hermits is not able to wipe himself altogether out of the memories of men. This did not occur to Miller, and he hatched one of the most extraordinary plots that has ever emanated from a criminal's brain.

One afternoon he waited for Mr. Huelin in the house in Wellington Square. The repairs were nearing completion, but as yet a suitable tenant had not been found, and it seemed that the place would remain empty for weeks. It was a substantial building with brick walls, and to the plasterer it seemed to have been made for such a job as he was now contemplating.

Mr. Huelin arrived and walked into the back room where Miller was pretending to finish his day's work. The two men were alone; one elderly and somewhat feeble; the other young, and possessed of a frame which the ravages of drink had not entirely weakened. There could have been only one end to a contest between such a pair, even if conducted on fair lines. But Miller was not going to fight according to the rules. There was too much at stake, and he waited until the clergyman's back was turned. Then he struck him down, and before the old man could cry out he strangled him. There was no struggle, and Mr. Huelin could not have done more than emit a weak cry for help. Not a sound penetrated the walls, and the dwellers in the square were quite ignorant of what was happening. Most of them knew Mr. Huelin by sight, and his aversion from making acquaintances was understood. He liked to go his own way unobserved and not interfered with, and they left it at that.

It was Miller's first crime, but he acted with all the self-assurance and callousness that are supposed to distinguish the professional criminal. There was, of course, the chance that at any moment some one might ring the bell and ask to be shown over the house, but he was not nervous or apprehensive. He had convinced himself that his plans would not miscarry, and he was buoyed up by the knowledge that a fortune was awaiting him at 15, Paulton Square. He knew that he would not have to run any risks by forging cheques or selling paper money. Gold could not be traced, and he would not have to answer any awkward questions when he tendered the sovereigns and half-sovereigns belonging to his victim. Banknotes would have rendered his chances of escape remote. A working man does not usually receive his wages in five pound notes, and Miller was cute enough to recognise this. He was out for gold and silver —both untraceable.

He concealed the body of the unfortunate clergyman in a drain in the house. As a practical bricklayer it was easy enough for the murderer to make the necessary excavation, and he succeeded in hiding the body with the minimum of trouble. His object, of course, was to avert suspicion by not disturbing the outward appearance of the empty house. But the murder of Mr. Huelin was in reality only part of the task he had set himself. The faithful housekeeper stood like a sentry between him and his victim's hoard, and now Miller went to Paulton Square to complete his plans. It is amazing to think that the fellow actually plotted in cold blood to murder two persons on the same day and in different places in a crowded part of London, oblivious of the risk of detection, and only possessed of one idea—the stealing of the money Mr. Huelin was in the habit of keeping at home.

Ann Boss, the housekeeper, opened the door to him. She knew Miller by now as one of her master's employes, and when he informed her that he had been sent by Mr. Huelin to examine the walls with a view to doing certain repairs she offered no objection to admitting him to the house.

For a second time that day Miller found himself alone with a person whom he had resolved to murder. This time his task was easier, for he had only a woman to deal with. The poor creature, implicitly trusting the scoundrel, followed him into the kitchen quite unconscious of her doom, never to know that her employer's economy was the direct cause of her death. Had Mr. Huelin given the housekeeper another woman to assist her, the double crime would have been impossible, but as it was, once he had separated the opposing forces, Walter Miller knew that they had no chance against him.

Here again, had some one called—tradesman's boy, beggar, circular distributor, canvasser—in fact, any one of the innumerable persons who help to make or mar life in the suburbs—a life might have been saved, but there was no one to interpose, and Miller, now mad with the blood lust, killed her without the slightest compunction.

It was getting late, and as he was anxious to "make a night of it" he hastily threw some clothes over the housekeeper's body, and began his search for the money for which he had taken the two lives. It was not long before he was rewarded, and, having filled his pockets, he left the house and went off to the West End.

At last he was rich, and could spend freely. No longer was it necessary to count every coin before he made a purchase, and when in the Haymarket he met a young woman of his acquaintance he took her to a restaurant, and afterwards to a music hall, spending money on the principle of the man who is satisfied only with the best.

It was a time of great political excitement in London. France and Prussia were fighting desperately, and as British sympathies were with France it took all the skill of the Government to keep the country out of the war. The theatres and music halls reflected the popular excitement, and for these and other reasons the wealthy working man was not so noticeable as he might have been in more ordinary times. Once a policeman touched the murderer on the arm and roughly ordered him to keep quiet. With a hoarse laugh of defiance Miller passed on with the girl clinging to his arm, too intoxicated to realise the narrow escape he had had.

But when the night of riotous, unreasoning, and false happiness passed, Miller awoke to face the problem of disposing of the body of the housekeeper. He had a vague notion that if he managed to get rid of it he would be able to take up his residence at 15, Paulton Square, and live there in luxury. If that was impossible he would sell it and disappear. Mr. Huelin had no friends and his absence would be attributed to a sudden desire to travel. The foreign name of the unfortunate clergyman suggested that he was more than ordinarily interested in the life-and-death struggle going on in the land of his forefathers.

"I'll tell them that Mr. Huelin's in France, said Miller, as he debated the subject. "But there's that woman's body to be hid first."

The curious feature of the whole sordid crime is that Miller apparently only once gave way to fright, and this was at the very last moment. During the days he was spending his victim's money not once did the spectre of retribution appear to him. A more remarkable instance of callousness can scarcely be found. It is not clear whether he told his girl friend or not of the means by which he had obtained his wealth. Perhaps she suspected that it was the proceeds of a burglary, though there is a suspicion that in his drunken state he gave her a hint of the truth. Whatever happened she resolved to stand by him as long as the money lasted.

Miller's final decision was to pack the body in a box and have it taken to a house in Fulham, also the property of the clergyman. This was an empty house in a somewhat isolated position and there he intended to bury the corpse and leave it for ever. Every hour it remained at Paulton Square there was a risk of discovery. In addition to that he wanted to reside there himself undisturbed until he disposed of the contents.

He placed the body of the housekeeper in a wooden box, and tied it up with strong cord. It was, of course, impossible for him to remove it unaided, but he did not shrink from completing his plans. With incredible daring the moment he had got the box and its ghastly contents ready, he actually engaged an old woman to come and act as housekeeper and to wait on himself and the girl he had brought to share his fortune. The old woman knew nothing of the double murder. It was the demeanour of the younger woman that imposed upon the newly-installed housekeeper, who was given to understand that her employer was a workman who had unexpectedly inherited a fortune.

Another day of dissipation followed, and the many publicans in the neighbourhood of Piccadilly changed sovereigns which Mr. Huelin had hoarded for years, little dreaming of their origin. The young woman was an able guide to the most expensive pleasures, and for a time Miller was convinced that crime did pay, and that it was worth the risk when one could exchange a life of toil for one of ease. There is no doubt that he had a large capacity for enjoying himself, and the wonder is that he followed his trade for such a long time before breaking the bonds and becoming an out and out criminal.

Yet there was always a spectre at the feast, and there was the pressing problem of the disposal of the housekeeper's body. Half a dozen times Miller was on the point of employing a carter to take it to the house in Fulham, but his courage always failed him at the last moment. He wanted to remain as long as possible in the West End, where he could forget that Paulton Square and Wellington Square existed.

But with the new housekeeper on the premises there came a time when he must rid the place of its encumbrance, and having examined the box carefully in the company of his companion he announced to her that on the following day they would see the last of it, and henceforth they would never be reminded of his terrible crimes.

Miller had, after much deliberation, decided to give the job to a vanman of the name of Piper. The latter was a powerful man who could, with Miller's aid, carry the box to the van, thus limiting the number called in to help in the removal of the corpse. Besides, he had a shrewd idea that Piper would never suspect that anything was wrong. To confirm this he stood him a drink in the bar-room of a Chelsea public house, where, having studied his man, he came to the conclusion that Piper was not likely to ask awkward questions. But even with all these precautions Miller was beginning to feel that escape was not so certain as he had thought. He had plenty of money left, and he told his companion that it would be a tragedy indeed, if he was arrested before he had time to spend it. They, therefore, resolved on another night in the West End before they ran the risk of all. The removal of the box would result in arrest or escape. They were staking their all on it, and they needed something to stiffen their courage for the ordeal before them.

When the wretched couple reached Piccadilly Circus, Miller made an excuse and left the girl for a few minutes. She saw him enter a chemist's shop, but on his return to her side he did not tell her what he had purchased. In his waistcoat pocket, however, there now reposed a small phial containing laudanum. Walter Miller was prepared to cheat the law if disaster happened the next day. He did not show any sign of fear, and the girl had no reason to suspect that her laughing, apparently happy friend was actually contemplating suicide. Seated in the dress circle of a West End music hall they joined in the choruses, and Miller was so exuberant as to attract the attention of the official, vulgarly termed the chucker out. The respectable members of the audience regarded him as an illiterate man driven to drink by an unexpected fortune. They were right to a certain extent, but they never suspected that they were rubbing shoulders with a murderer.

Every murderer, no matter what his position or education, is distinguished by a certain mixture of cunning and simplicity which eventually leads to discomfiture. For a man who had little or no schooling, Miller behaved with a certain cleverness which was no doubt brought out by the circumstances he found himself in. He behaved as one who had nothing to conceal. There was no slinking down side streets or dismal periods of self-imprisonment until darkness set in and enabled him to emerge into the streets. Those who knew Walter Miller by sight—and they were accustomed to see him drinking when men in his trade were working hard—had little cause for suspicion. His idleness was notorious, and his ability to pay for his own beer was nothing unusual. Miller had the reputation of raising money by ingenious methods and that was why in Chelsea his affluence created no gossip.

It must have been a terribly anxious moment for him when the vanman's knock was heard on the door. The crisis was approaching, and on the next few minutes would depend the issue of life and death. Miller was certain that if he only got the box into the van unquestioned the rest would be easy. Would Piper ask questions? Would he suspect anything from the unusual weight of the box? Miller had already warned him that the contents were heavy, so Piper ought not to grumble at that.

It was probably Miller's idea that if he had the box removed in the daylight there would be less cause for anxiety on the ground of arousing suspicion. The vanman would take it as an ordinary job, and would get it over as soon as possible for the sake of the good price Miller was paying him. The chances seemed to be in favour of success.

The old woman admitted Piper, and took him into the front room where the box was standing. Here Miller and the young woman received him on the surface calm, but inwardly anxious and fearful.

The vanman stooped to examine the fastenings.

"Cord a bit loose," he said, curtly, and stretched out his hand as if to tighten it. Instantly Miller interposed.

"It's all right," he said gruffly. "I know a bit about making a knot. Give me a hand and we'll carry the box out. You'll find the cords all right. Anyhow, I'm not going to let you touch them. I'm in a hurry."

He must have spoken with greater heat than was necessary, but even then he did not arouse the suspicions of the other man. Piper was only annoyed that his judgment should be doubted. He had spent a life-time in his trade, and he had handled thousands of boxes of all shapes and sizes, and to be told that he was ignorant of the art of packing irritated him. He would not take lessons from a mere plasterer, and he was obstinate in insisting upon having his own way.

"I wouldn't trust a box tied like that on my van," he said, bluntly. "It 'ud fall to bits. If you want it taken away you'd better let me fasten the cord."

Miller was determined to prevent him, but he was not quick enough. Piper, without waiting for permission, stooped over the box once more, and ran his hand along the side to test the cords.

"They're all loose," he said triumphantly. "Try them for yourself. I—" he stopped suddenly, as he saw his own hand. It was covered with blood.

For a moment or two not a word was spoken. Piper stood staring at his hand as though hypnotised. The old woman watched him, unable to believe the evidences of her senses. Miller's face went as white as the plaster of his trade, and the young woman who had shared his ill-gotten gains was transfixed with horror.

She broke the spell. With a cry of terror she rushed from the room into the street.

"What's in that box?" The inevitable question came, though Piper must have known the answer to it. Miller found his voice with difficulty, and, realising that he was in a corner, thought that a display of anger would frighten the vanman into complying with his wishes.

"You silly fool," he said contemptuously, "you've cut your hand and frightened the girl out of her life. Just you do as you're told or I'll get some one else for the job."

But Piper was not such a fool as Miller thought. The vanman knew that he had stumbled on a tragedy.

"That box must be opened at once," he said firmly, "and I won't let you leave the room until I see where the blood came from."

The murderer knew that the worst had happened, and now he stood facing the angry, suspicious face of the very man he had carefully chosen as being the best suited to his purpose.

"Will you open that box or must I?" The question came like a threat. Miller still held his ground, but he was possessed by an unreasoning fear now. His hand stole to the waistcoat pocket where the phial of laudanum rested. It was to be used when all hope was gone. Was there a chance left? Had the end of his days of riotous pleasure come?

The young woman had left the door half open. Miller turned and looked at it and then at the vanman again. Outside, pedestrians passed and repassed. Piper noticed them too, and was relieved, for there would be plenty of help near if he was forced to call for it.

Suddenly Miller sprang at the door. Piper, fearing that it was the preliminary movement to an attack on him, started back, but instantly saw his error. Miller was making a dash for freedom, and the vanman immediately darted after him.

Only a few paces separated them when they reached the square. Piper twice caught him by the arm, to be shaken off each time. But when the pursuer raised his voice a crowd gathered and joined in the hunt, and a couple of hundred yards away a policeman closed in upon the flying murderer and in his powerful grip Miller was helpless.

Piper hurriedly made his explanation to the officer, and accompanied him and his prisoner back to the house. Here they were joined by half a dozen constables, summoned by whistle, and whilst three of them kept the crowd at bay the others entered to test the statement Piper had made.

Of course, it was merely the matter of a few moments to reveal the contents of the box and to discover the first clues towards the double crime. Miller knew he was doomed, and taking advantage of the general excitement, he swallowed the contents of the laudanum phial. It did not, however, have any effect, for an emetic was hastily administered, and the prisoner was then conveyed to the police station.

Miller sullenly refused to render the authorities any aid, although he did not trouble to deny his guilt. But the police soon found the body of the clergyman. It was known that Miller had been employed in untenanted houses belonging to the deceased, and accordingly the detectives made a systematic search of every unoccupied house on his estate, stopping only when they found the body in the drain at No. 25, Wellington Square.

To say that the news created a sensation is to mildly describe the excitement and horror of the public when they heard of the fate of the clergyman and his housekeeper. The double crime proved that even in a densely-populated suburb there is little protection from the murderer prepared to take some amount of risk.

There was no question as to Miller's guilt. He scarcely disputed the accuracy of the charge against him, and he behaved with indifference, consoling himself with the reflection that he had had a run for his money, and that if the horse he had backed had not won it had come very near landing a big stake for him. The magistrates committed him for trial, and when the prisoner appeared at Old Bailey he had the services of counsel.

The only defence was a plea of insanity. Counsel argued that no sane man would have behaved as Walter Miller had, but, if some of his acts were extraordinary, others indicated that he was possessed of a cunning and clear thinking brain, and that he was a man of more than ordinary intelligence. He had planned the two murders with consummmate daring, and yet all the time had been more or less cautious. A lunatic might have murdered an old clergyman, but he would hardly have proceeded to slay the only dangerous person left and take possession of the victim's house. The employment of another housekeeper was a master-stroke, and there is good cause for the belief that if Piper, the vanman, had removed the box without having had his suspicions aroused, Miller would have avoided detection for many months, at any rate.

The young woman was not placed on trial, and when Miller heard the sentence of death, a warder stood on either side of him to prevent him making another attempt to commit suicide. Then he disappeared from public view, never to be seen again, save by those officials who were required by law to witness the execution.

The trial of Henry and Thomas Wainwright for the murder of Harriet Lane was the greatest murder trial over which Cockburn presided. The story is well known, and it is still talked of, though it is more than forty years since Henry Wainwright, owing to his incredible folly, was actually arrested with portions of his victim's remains in his possession.

It was a ghastly crime, and, taking place as it did in the squalid region of Whitechapel Road in the East End of London, it excited a horror which invested the tragedy with an atmosphere of repulsive and loathsome mystery.

A year had elapsed between the murder of Harriet Lane and the arrest of the man who had done her to death—a year Wainwright had spent in drinking in a vain effort to drown his remorse. His victim had lain buried in his workshop for twelve months when he attempted to remove her body, and he secured the assistance of a man of the name of Stokes to help him to carry the ghastly parcel. Stokes was tempted to examine the contents of the parcel, and his discovery that it contained a human head caused him to inform the police, and Wainwright was arrested. His brother Thomas, who was subsequently sentenced to seven years' penal servitude as an accessory after the act, was also captured.

The murderer had a very impressive trial, conducted with all the due regard for the impressive majesty of the law. The case for the prosecution was, of course, an overwhelming one, and yet the prisoner bore himself with courage, and when the final verdict was pronounced and he realised he was a doomed man, he said to the court :

" I will only say, standing as I do now upon the brink of eternity, that I swear I am not the murderer of the remains found in my possession. I swear that I never fired a pistol in my life. I swear also that I did not bury the mutilated remains, nor did I exhume them."

It was an obvious lie, framed in a desperate effort to stave off inevitable doom, and the Lord Chief Justice, before passing sentence, replied briefly to the prisoner's declaration, pointing out that the evidence had been most convincing, and that the very nature of the crime made any hope of a reprieve a delusion.

Wainwright maintained an obstinate air of injured innocence until the day before his execution. Then he admitted that he deserved his fate, but he gave the prison chaplain to understand that he alone was not to blame.

Henry Wainwright was a confirmed smoker, and he gave the authorities no trouble as long as he was allowed a smoke. On the last night of his life he sat up late enjoying a good cigar, and the soothing weed enabled him to steady his nerves, which had suffered greatly by his over-indulgence in intoxicating drinks.

Cockburn's selection to represent the British Government at Geneva when the claims of the United States of America over the depredations of the *Alabama* were arbitrated upon was a well-deserved honour. The American representatives pressed their country's claims with a zeal that bordered on unfairness, and Cockburn found himself unable to agree with the majority decision of the arbitrators. He published a report of his own, setting forth his reasons, and when passions had cooled down it was generally agreed that the award to the United States was greater than that country should have got.

The *Alabama* was an armed ship, which was equipped in an English dockyard and allowed to leave British waters and prey upon ships belonging to North America. It was at the time of the American Civil War, and the *Alabama* did tremendous havoc on behalf of the South.

It was admitted that Great Britain ought not to have permitted the ship to leave port, and this country was held responsible for the damage. However, by a strange freak of the arbitrators, the amount awarded was in excess of the damage done.

The Lord Chief Justice was a splendid linguist and devoted to literary work. He did not know what idleness was, and on the day he died he presided over the Court for Crown Cases Reserved.

Returning home after the rising of the court he had dinner, and then went to his study to complete a literary task he was engaged upon, but near midnight he suddenly collapsed at his desk, and he was found dead by his butler.

It was such a finish as he would have desired had the choice been left to him, for Sir Alexander Cockburn's genius was "an infinite capacity for taking pains," and he loved work for its own sake as much as for the success it brought him.

CHAPTER X

Lord Chief Baron Pollock

Sir Frederick Pollock, one of the greatest judges of his time, was remarkable for his learning, both legal and scientific, and his stately presence on the Bench was in accordance with the majesty and dignity of the law he administered. No one looking at the fine, intellectual face would have guessed that he was the son of a Windsor tradesman, but his father was David Pollock, a saddler, who was one of George III's favourite tradesmen, and had three sons, all of whom achieved considerable fame. They are now known in history as Sir David Pollock, Chief Justice of Bombay; Field Marshal Sir George Pollock, who performed great deeds in the Afghan campaign of 1848; and Sir Frederick Pollock, the subject of this chapter.

When we remember that the saddler's descendants in the third and fourth generations were, and are, notable men in the church, the law, literature, and the State, it will be conceded that Pollock and success go hand-in-hand.

The future Lord Chief Baron was called to the Bar in 1807 after completing a distinguished career at Cambridge, where he wound up as senior wrangler. At the Bar he quickly came to the front rank, and became, of course, a member of Parliament—for Huntingdon—and Attorney-General. Then in 1844 he was raised to the Bench, and for twenty-two years he was one of the busiest of judges, and scores of notable cases came before him. So many trials are celebrated in legal annals that it is difficult to make a selection, but at least four sensational murders call for mention.

His first great trial was that of the Mannings, for the murder of O'Connor. It was a very remarkable affair, and after the lapse of years still remains unique in many respects.

Maria Manning was a Swiss who had been a lady's maid before marrying her husband, a retired railway official, who was aware of her intimacy with a person of the name of O'Connor. Maria had lived in luxury whilst in service, and had saved a fairly decent sum of money, for she believed that the continental system prevailed in England, and that no girl could find a husband unless she had a *dot*.

With two men anxious to marry her, Maria took a few days to consider their proposals, but all she wished to know was which of them was the better off. Manning spent money freely, and, therefore, seemed the more prosperous, and the fact that he had been for years in the service of a great railway company was in his favour. On the other hand, O'Connor was only a dock worker who earned uncertain wages; yet he was a miser, and misers are notoriously rich; at least, Maria believed them to be.

Eventually, however, she married G. F. Manning, who "talked her over" by declaring that he had a good pension from the company, and so they became man and wife, and went to live in Miniver Place, Bermondsey.

It was a dismal change for Maria after the splendours of the ducal mansion she had resided in when maid to Lady Blantyre, the daughter of the Duchess of Sutherland, and when she discovered that her husband was practically penniless and that he drank immoderately she was bitterly disappointed. In vain she tried to protect her own savings from him; he took them by force and spent them in drink and in presents to other women. And, to crown all, Maria found out that O'Connor, the despised dock worker, was actually a rich man, having a large sum invested in first-class securities.

Despite the blighting of his hopes, O'Connor often came to Miniver Place to dine with the newly-married pair, Manning offering no objection, being content to share in the presents of money his wife's friend made her.

Sometimes Maria would go to O'Connor's lodgings, and once in a careless moment he showed her a lot of share certificates, which made the woman's mouth water. It afforded the dock worker keen pleasure now to be able to prove to her that she had made a mistake in rejecting a hard-working, saving man and accepting a drunkard.

But Maria quickly decided to get possession of O'Connor's fortune, and in her greed and covetousness she took her husband into her confidence. He was a weak-spirited creature—drink had made him that—and Maria had to use many arguments to persuade him to join in the plot. Twice O'Connor came to the house in Miniver Place, and on each occasion the Mannings had previously arranged to murder him, but at the last moment Manning had drawn back. The third time, however, was to pay for all.

The woman invited O'Connor to dine with her and her husband on the 9th of August, 1849, and as the Irishman was crossing London Bridge on his way to Miniver Place that afternoon he met two friends to whom he confided the name of his hostess. They were the last persons to see him alive, and it was that chance meeting which provided the first clue towards the elucidation of the subsequent murder mystery.

Never was a cold-blooded murder more carefully planned, and that a woman should have been mainly responsible for it is astounding.

Maria Manning purchased the pistol with which the deed was done, while her husband bought lime in which to bury the body of their victim, Manning having first ascertained that this particular lime would eat away the flesh. Then husband and wife dug a deep hole in the basement, and just as they were finishing a knock sounded on the hall door, and Maria ran upstairs to admit her visitor.

With a girlish giggle she told him that she had prepared a lovely goose for dinner, and that there was plenty to drink; but O'Connor was not to touch food or drink again in his life. The siren invited him to step downstairs, no doubt giving him to understand that they were to have dinner in the basement, and just as he was entering the room where his grave was he was shot in the head and immediately afterwards attacked with a hammer.

There was no struggle, and it was not long before the murderers had covered up the body, and had endeavoured to conceal the fact that the ground had recently been dug. Then they sat down and made a good meal off the roast goose, and, apparently, enjoyed themselves thoroughly.

A few days later a friend of O'Connor's called to inquire about him. He had not been seen since the ninth. Did Mrs. Manning know anything about him? She admitted that he had dined with her on the date mentioned, but he had left the house quite well, and she anxiously expressed the hope that nothing had happened to him.

Several days passed, and the man's friends became alarmed. They went to the police, and declared that Mrs. Manning ought to know more than anybody else. The police first called on O'Connor's landlady, who said that Mrs. Manning had been to her lodger's rooms after the ninth. It scarcely surprised them then that a search of the rooms should result in the discovery that O'Connor's savings had been stolen.

The police now journeyed to Miniver Place, but there they found an empty house. Every stick of furniture had been removed, and the Mannings had flown and not a single person knew their whereabouts.

Of course, a search was instituted for the body, and at last the basement grave was discovered, and the skeleton of the murdered man brought to light. But there was so little flesh on the bones that it would have been impossible to have identified it to the satisfaction of a jury had not the luck been on the side of the police.

O'Connor had been fitted with a set of false teeth, and it was found intact in the mouth, the lime having failed to destroy it. When the dentist who had supplied the teeth came forward and identified the set as one he had supplied to O'Connor, there was no doubt as to the identity of the corpse, and the hue and cry began for the obvious murderers.

They had separated after leaving the house, Maria travelling to Edinburgh and Manning to Jersey, but, despite the lack of information concerning their movements, the police were able to trace both within a very short space of time. The woman was taken whilst trying to deal in share certificates belonging to O'Connor, and Manning was arrested in a drunken condition in a Jersey hotel, where his conduct had aroused suspicion.

The trial before Lord Chief Baron Pollock attracted enormous crowds, and when the remarkable character of Maria Manning began to be known the struggle to obtain even a glimpse of her became the daily ambition of thousands.

She bore herself throughout the ordeal with haughtiness and contempt, the latter mainly being directed against her husband. Not once did she falter, and counsel, witnesses, and even the judge himself came in for a share of her biting criticisms. The Chief Baron had a strenuous time, but never once did his singular courtesy fail or his learning and wisdom desert him.

Maria swore that her husband alone was responsible, but no one believed that this obviously strong-minded woman had been influenced for a moment by the crawling, nervous wreck who stood beside her in the dock. He made a miserable show, whining for mercy and feebly protesting his innocence until the whole court was sick of him.

When sentence of death was pronounced Mrs. Manning became hysterical and abusive, but was quickly removed. In the cells she regained her composure, and informed the wardress that she would not be hanged, as she had very powerful friends. That night she wrote a long letter to the Duchess of Sutherland asking her to intervene on her behalf.

When she received no answer she wrote to

Queen Victoria. Again she was disappointed, and when she realised that her epistolary efforts were in vain she turned to the woman who was guarding her in the condemned cell and said, "The Queen is no lady. I am surprised at her."

The public execution of the murderers was marked by a "death-bed" reconciliation between husband and wife.

Trembling with terror, Manning asked her to forgive him, and as a sign that she did so she kissed him. The woman wore a black satin dress, having insisted on being dressed in "genteel fashion," and, of course, the prison authorities offered no objection. But this last appearance of Maria Manning had disastrous consequences for the trade in that material. For many years afterwards no woman would think of wearing black satin, which had become such a startling reminder of a most horrible crime, and consequently thousands of persons were thrown out of work, and numerous small traders went bankrupt.

The trial of Franz Muller, the young German, for the murder of Mr. Thomas Briggs on the North London Railway, was another of Pollock's experiences on the Bench. There were features of this crime which made for a world-wide interest.

Railways were practically in their infancy, and critics who sighed for the old stage-coach days, which they could remember, declared that the murder of Mr. Briggs was proof positive that railways were a danger to the State! Very foolish, no doubt, but we are over fifty years wiser nowadays.

Muller travelled with Mr. Briggs, who was a bank cashier, with the intention of robbing him, and attacked him shortly after the train had left Hackney Wick station. He succeeded in partially stunning him and throwing him from the train. Then he concealed the gold watch and chain of his victim, and as the train was entering Bow station hastily picked up what he supposed to be his hat and decamped.

When Mr. Briggs' body was found on the line he was unconscious, but he never recovered, and twenty-four hours later was dead.

It was a strange coincidence that the finding of blood in the carriage where the struggle took place should have been made by two young men who were clerks in the same bank as Mr. Briggs. Besides the bloodstains they found a handbag, a stick, and a hat. And the hat was not the one Mr. Briggs had worn. As was the fashion then, he had worn a tall hat, but this one was lower in the crown, and showed signs of having been cut down, a custom amongst those second-hand traders who supplied headgear to cabmen.

Inside this particular hat was the name of the original maker, and the police, starting from this point, traced the hat to Franz Muller, who had lodged with a cabman for some time. But when the detectives wished to question the German they found that he had started for America on a sailing ship.

Detectives from Scotland Yard, accompanied by the witnesses necessary to identify Muller, travelled by a steamer, and actually landed in New York three weeks before Muller's ship was sighted. When it came into port the officers went aboard, effected the arrest, and found amongst his luggage the hat and watch belonging to Mr. Briggs.

During the three weeks the party from England had been waiting for the arrival of the *Victoria*, the ship Muller had sailed in, New York had become intensely excited over the chase.

All the time in Britain the papers had little else to fill their columns with, and now, although the United States were in the throes of a civil war, Muller threatened to oust from public interest the deeds of the warriors on both sides. The murderer resisted extradition proceedings, but, of course, was promptly handed over to the English authorities and taken back to London.

Meanwhile a new force had arisen in London to look after the interests of the accused. This was the "German Legal Protection Society," which was formed by a collection of Germans residing in the metropolis, whose actions in the matter seem to have been based on the assumption that the cowardly murder of an old man by a young German ought not to be visited with the just punishment of the law.

They tried to draw a herring across the path of the natural resentment against the criminal by asserting that the prosecution of Muller was inspired by political spite. Prussia had just robbed Denmark of the Schleswig-Holstein provinces, an act which had been censured by every freedom-loving Briton, and the "German Legal Protection Society" said that Muller ought not to be charged with murder simply because he happened to belong to the nation which had recently displeased Great Britain.

A large sum of money was subscribed for Muller's legal expenses, and Mr. Serjeant Parry, then at the height of his fame, was the leading counsel engaged.

The Government, however, sent down to the Old Bailey Sir Robert Collier, the Solicitor-General, Mr. Serjeant Ballantine, Mr. Hannen—afterwards the President of the Divorce Court

—and Mr. Hardinge Giffard, later Earl of Halsbury and Lord Chancellor of England, to prosecute—a formidable legal team, which proved how seriously the authorities regarded the case.

With Lord Chief Baron Pollock and Baron Martin as the presiding judges there could be no doubt of the fairness of the trial. The defence was permitted every license, but it is surprising, considering how strong the evidence of guilt was, that the trial should have occupied three days.

Of course Muller protested that he was innocent. Once he was told that his fellow-countrymen in London were convinced of their ability to secure his acquittal he posed as an injured innocent. He must have known that conviction was certain, but he hoped for a reprieve. For that reason he refrained from confessing until the moment the noose was actually round his neck.

Pollock's summing-up shivered to atoms all the well-built-up theories of counsel for the defence. He laid impartially before the jury the facts on either side, and in the fairest manner indicated the overwhelming strength of the circumstantial evidence. A quarter of an hour sufficed for the jury to decide, and when the verdict of guilty was announced Baron Martin sentenced the murderer to death.

"The German Legal Protection Society" instantly summoned all its forces for a sort of grand assault on British justice. Deputations of square-headed Prussians with unspeakable names thronged the Home Secretary's office. A reprieve was called for, and a petition got up in favour of it, but very few decent persons appended their signatures.

The Germans, however, had no difficulty in securing the interest of the then King of Prussia and a host of minor Prussian princes, who, in the intervals of dodging their creditors, did not mind taking part in a discussion of which they knew nothing. The papers were deluged with letters, and all the usual tricks characteristic of the Germans resorted to. Much political capital was made out of the affair, and the society succeeded in obtaining the support of nearly every German in London. Their greatest achievement was that of making the King of Prussia telegraph direct to Queen Victoria at the last moment, requesting her to save Muller from the hangman. But there was never any danger of the cowardly ruffian escaping his just doom. The Home Secretary consulted Lord Chief Baron Pollock, and it was mainly on his recommendation that a reprieve was refused. The murderer was executed publicly, and at the last moment confessed his guilt to the German chaplain who attended him on the scaffold.

The murder of Mrs. Elmsley by James Mullins was a tragedy that for a few days made an obscure street in Stepney a Mecca for thousands of Londoners who would not in any other circumstances have thought of approaching that somewhat unsavoury thoroughfare. The crime is remarkable, because it was unwittingly solved by an informer, who was surprised at being arrested and charged with the crime which he had laid at the door of another man, who was, of course, innocent.

Mrs. Elmsley was a woman who owned some property in Stepney, and Mullins was a workman employed by her to effect certain repairs. She ived alone in a house, looking after it herself, though occasionally she indulged in the luxury of a charwoman. One morning she was not seen by her neighbours, and when the house was forcibly entered she was found dead, her head having been battered in.

The news spread like wildfire that Sunday morning, and by the afternoon the street was thronged. The police were early on the scene, but while two men were suspected, there was not sufficient evidence to justify the arrest of either. Then James Mullins came forward and volunteered the information that a certain individual of his acquaintance, who happened to be Mrs. Elmsley's agent, had murdered her and had concealed part of the booty in a disused brickfield. The detectives listened with interest, and readily agreed to accompany Mullins to the spot where he said he had seen the murderer bury the stolen goods. Everything was arranged with great care—Mullins insisted upon that—and evincing considerable enjoyment of his own cleverness, he brought the police to the scene of the buried booty. Sure enough a parcel containing articles belonging to the murdered woman was found, and the inspector took charge of it before proceeding to arrest the agent who had been denounced. Then with Mullins following in the rear, his eyes gleaming with greed as he anticipated the reward, the party returned to the police station. The informer was in the best of spirits, but he had been too clever.

The police inspector had been somewhat puzzled by his demeanour. He seemed to know too much about the whole affair to be quite innocent of all participation in the crime, and at this point he undoubtedly suspected him of having been an accomplice. For a few minutes the inspector was occupied giving directions as to the disposal of the man he had arrested. Then he turned to Mullins, and immediately informed him that he was a prisoner, too. Mullins nearly collapsed. Guilt could be read in his evil face. Stammeringly he swore that a terrible mistake was being made. The inspector merely ordered him to be taken to the cells.

When Mullins had gone he revealed to his subordinates the reason for this dramatic turn to recent events. The inspector had noticed that the bootlace which had been used to bind up the parcel of stolen goods matched those worn by Mullins. It was a small coincidence perhaps, but well worth close attention.

The next stage in the drama was at the Old Bailey, where Lord Chief Baron Pollock, in robes of scarlet, presided, and James Mullins stood shivering in the dock. The agent had been released at once, and, despite a few setbacks, the police were able to come into court with full proofs. There was practically no defence, for Mullins had not been able to get rid of the weapon with which the deed had been done, and there were several conclusive pieces of circumstantial evidence which proved the guilt of the accused.

A packed court saw the wretch in the dock crumple up as counsel for the prosecution drove home his guilt, and when, after the only possible verdict, Mullins was piteously asking for mercy, few could listen unmoved to the sentence of death.

It was the circumstances leading up to the crime that excited the interest of Londoners. Mrs. Elmsley was said to have kept hidden in her house a very large sum of money, and

Mullins murdered her, thinking that he would find sufficient money to make him rich for life. But the crime brought him practically nothing, and he went to his death like the coward that he was.

Another London tragedy, two years after the trial of Mullins, was not so satisfactorily cleared up. In 1862 a sweep named Gardner and his wife lived in Northumberland Alley, Fenchurch Street, right in the heart of the City of London. They had a young servant girl who was on more than friendly terms with Gardner, and naturally Mrs. Gardner objected to their intimacy. There were constant quarrels between the couple, culminating in the death of the wife, who was found lying on the floor of her bedroom one night with her throat cut and a razor in her right hand.

The doctor who was called in immediately, was examining the body when Gardner, in a great state of agitation, entered, and with appropriate expressions of dismay knelt by the body and at once took the knife from his dead wife's hand. This was regarded with suspicion by the doctor, who had already decided for himself that the weapon had been placed in the woman's hand after death.

On his report Gardner was arrested when fiercely asserting his innocence. He swore that his wife must have committed suicide. Then, when that was proved to have been impossible, he accused the servant girl of the crime. She was arrested, but shortly afterwards set at liberty to be the principal witness at the trial.

It must be said that the evidence for the prosecution, although presented with great skill by Mr. H. Poland—now Sir Harry Poland, K.C.

—was hardly strong enough to justify a verdict, and the almost universal opinion was that the jury would either disagree or acquit.

There was a great deal made of Mrs. Gardner's unhappy life with her husband, and the prosecution emphasised the fact that the servant girl could hardly have succeeded in cutting Mrs. Gardner's throat without the woman having made a desperate struggle, and there were no signs of a fight for life having taken place. Gardner, on the other hand, was a strong, healthy man, who could have easily murdered her without giving her a chance to struggle.

The weakness of the defence was Gardner's change of front. First he said his wife had taken her own life; then he had turned against the servant girl and denounced her as being guilty. He was able to supply his counsel with scraps of conversation which tended to prove his accusations.

He swore that the girl had declared that she would never leave the house again, and that if it came to a question as to which of them went—Mrs. Gardner or herself—the sweep's wife must go. This was interpreted to mean that the girl meant to murder her mistress.

If Mr. Poland, as he then was, had not exercised his right to say the last word—the privilege of counsel for the prosecution—Gardner would never have been convicted. But in his final speech the great barrister smashed the defence, and although the jury took an hour and a half to come to a decision, it was against the accused when the twelve good men and true returned into court. Gardner passionately swore that he was innocent, and his words were evidently so spontaneous and sincere that they created a distinct impression in his favour.

The Lord Chief Baron pronounced sentence of death, and the prisoner disappeared, but there was a general feeling that, after all, a mistake might have been made. The foreman of the jury had strongly recommended the accused to mercy, an odd proceeding in face of the verdict, for the crime had been a most brutal one; but the jury thought that the murder had been committed in a passion, though even that hardly justified an appeal for mercy for the convict.

The judge, however, took care to forward the recommendation of the jury to the Home Secretary, and, when asked for advice, declared that it was a case for reprieve. Consequently Gardner was sent to penal servitude, the reprieve convincing a great many of the public that the very highest authorities were of opinion that there was a doubt as to the guilt of the accused. This is always unsatisfactory, as it is obviously undesirable to condemn a man to lifelong imprisonment on the ground of mere suspicion.

Gardner survived his sentence, though when he emerged into the world again it was to find that a great change had taken place in it. The judge who had tried him was dead, but his son sat on the Bench, and the ex-convict, friendless and alone, was helped by a charitable society to emigrate to Australia. There he married again, and died fairly well off.

In 1866 Sir Frederick Pollock retired from the Bench. He was then eighty-three, but in full possession of his faculties. The Queen rewarded him with a baronetcy, and he lived to enjoy it four years, eventually dying in 1870 at the great age of eighty-seven.

The judge married twice and had eighteen children, several of whom distinguished themselves, while of his grandchildren the best known are Dr. Bertram Pollock, once headmaster of Wellington College, and now Bishop of Norwich, and Sir Ernest Pollock, ex-Attorney-General.

CHAPTER XI

Sir Samuel Martin

Samuel Martin was an Ulster Irishman who came to London to seek his fortune, and as he attained the position of a Baron of Exchequer before he was fifty, he may be said to have found it sooner than most men. He was a popular and kind-hearted companion, but never lukewarm in his opinions, and he was seldom tender to criminals.

During his twenty years at the Bar, Martin earned the reputation of a sound commercial lawyer, but it was a racing dispute that made him known to the public. A horse, called "Bloomsbury," having won the Ascot Derby Stakes, payment of the stakes was refused on the ground that the owner had not described the animal properly when entering it. Mr. Ridsdale thereupon brought an action against the stewards, and Martin, by his skilful conduct of the case, secured the victory for his client.

This trial was one of the few in which the Irish barrister appeared which can be said to have been of general interest. As a rule he was engaged in dry-as-dust cases in foggy courts before somnolent judges, and it was not until he was promoted to the Bench in 1850 that he became a really prominent figure in public life. Before this occurred he became a Queen's Counsel, and for a few years was Member of Parliament for Pontefract.

Baron Martin was associated with numerous sensational trials, and he invariably escaped criticism, but once he made the mistake of taking sides too soon in a murder case, which eventually resulted in the person found guilty and sentenced to death being released with a "free pardon."

He had been nearly fifteen years on the Bench when, in February, 1865, he tried the Italian, Pelizzioni, who was accused of the murder of Michael Harrington. This affair, known as the Hatton Garden murder, created a great sensation and led to a diplomatic correspondence.

There seemed on the surface to be something romantic in the affair, though it was, after all, only the common story of a public-house brawl. A party of Englishmen and Italians met in the "Golden Anchor" public-house in Great Saffron Hill, the quarters of the Italian colony in London, and, having quarrelled in their cups, set to with knives and fists. The brief encounter led to three trials, two of them for murder, and one for attempted murder, and Baron Martin presided at the first.

The cause of the brawl was never known, and it lasted only a few minutes, being abruptly terminated by the discovery that one of the English participants, Harrington, had been stabbed and was unconscious. An alarm was raised, and two men seized Pelizzioni, who was actually lying on Harrington's prostrate body, a small knife clutched in his right hand.

The evidence against the prisoner was very strong. Witnesses swore that he was the only Italian who had been near Harrington at the moment the murderous assault had been committed, and, in addition, it was stated in court that when Harrington was dying in St.

Bartholomew's Hospital, Pelizzioni had been confronted by him and identified by Harrington as his assailant. These facts seemed to the judge to be conclusive.

The witnesses for the defence were a sorry lot, and beyond swearing that a cousin of the prisoner's, referred to as Gregorio, was the murderer, could do nothing to prove their contention. Baron Martin summed up strongly against the prisoner, the jury said "Guilty," and the accused was sentenced to death.

At this point a series of sensations began. Immediately the result of the trial was known, the Italian Ambassador called on the Home Secretary to discuss it; the leading Italian residents in London formed a committee to watch the interests of the condemned man, and private detectives, as well as the police of several cities, were employed to trace Gregorio, the man suspected to be the slayer of Harrington.

Thanks to the exertions of the Italian Ambassador, Pelizzioni was reprieved, but only just in time, for the hangman was on his way to Newgate when the Home Secretary's decision was conveyed to the governor of that gaunt old prison.

The arrest of Gregorio Mogni, to give him his full name, took place in Birmingham, and as he confessed at once to having stabbed Harrington, hardly any one doubted Pelizzioni's innocence. But the latter was held a prisoner in Newgate whilst Gregorio was tried for murder. Of course, Baron Martin took no part in the subsequent proceedings, but it is necessary to follow up the first trial, as it was his charge to the jury that had caused them to convict Pelizzioni. Gregorio pleaded "Not guilty," asserting that his offence was manslaughter and nothing more, and his counsel succeeded in gaining the adherence of the jury to this opinion. The Italian was sentenced to five years' penal servitude, and he was immediately taken to Millbank Penitentiary to undergo his punishment.

An extraordinary state of affairs now obtained. Two men had been found guilty of the same crime, and one was under sentence of death and in the condemned cell at Newgate, whilst the other was at Millbank. Even the police, who had displayed considerable animus against Pelizzioni, did not dispute the fact that Pelizzioni could not be guilty if Gregorio had killed Harrington, and it was thought that the authorities would release him from Newgate.

But the Home Secretary, influenced, I believe, by Baron Martin's attitude, declined to set Pelizzioni free, and he was kept a prisoner for some weeks while the law officers of the Crown made up their minds about him. Their decision was to place him on trial again, and this time he was charged with attempting to murder the potman of the "Golden Anchor," who, it was alleged, had been stabbed by Pelizzioni. There were two judges to try him, and a great array of counsel on either side, Mr. Hardinge Giffard leading for the prosecution. But the jury acquitted the prisoner, and soon afterwards he was given her Majesty's gracious pardon for the murder of Michael Harrington and released from prison.

The action of the responsible authorities in detaining Pelizzioni after the conviction of Gregorio Mogni unmistakably proved that there was a strong suspicion that trickery had been resorted to.

Sir Samuel Martin never believed that Pelizzioni was not the murderer of Harrington, and the evidence against the Italian at the first trial was overwhelming. The judge was reproved by the more popular papers for his one-sided summing-up on that occasion, but Sir Samuel did not change his opinion with advancing years. He, and others, too, thought that Gregorio, aware of the fact that if he were to confess to having stabbed Harrington in a *mêlée*, he would be found guilty of manslaughter only, came forward and risked a few years of penal servitude on his cousin's account.

Whatever the truth, it was a very puzzling affair altogether. It is almost unique for a man to be convicted of murder and to find himself free after a brief spell of imprisonment.

The Brighton poisoning mystery of 1871 is not forgotten yet, and certainly nothing like it is to be found in the chronicles of crime. That a woman of good birth and position should plan murder on a wholesale scale because she wished to prove herself guiltless of an attempt to poison a friend is astounding enough, but the circumstances leading up to Christiana Edmunds' crime were almost equally productive of amazement.

Miss Edmunds was living at Brighton with her widowed mother, a lady who could afford to live comfortably on her private means. Christiana had been well educated, and was not without good looks. But she grew tired of the quiet life she was leading, and it would have been wiser had she followed some form of employment. Her father had died a lunatic, and her brother had been an imbecile, so the Edmunds family was not healthy, and opportunities for brooding over her unloved condition were not good for Christiana.

Then one morning on the Brighton front she saw a gentleman who happened to glance at her. The girl thereupon decided that she had met her soul-mate, and for four consecutive days she haunted the "front" expectantly. She was with a friend when she met the handsome stranger again, and, to her joy, this friend was acquainted with the gentleman. An introduction ensued, and Christiana Edmunds knew that he was a local doctor.

It is not difficult to improve upon a casual introduction to a doctor. All one has to do is to be ill and send for him. Christiana Edmunds pursued the obvious course. She told her mother that she was out of sorts, and that she must see a doctor at once, and she spared her mother the trouble of deciding whom to call in by insisting that her friend, Dr. Beard, should be sent for.

The acquaintance between the two developed, and it was cemented by Mrs. Beard receiving Christiana. All the parties concerned were of equal social position, and there was nothing strange in one of the doctor's patients being a visitor to his house. But Christiana, who was madly in love with Dr. Beard, soon began to think of the time she hoped would come when he would be a widower, and in a position to propose to her.

She decided to assist nature to carry off Mrs. Beard, and the agency she selected was strychnine concealed in chocolate creams. She secured the deadly poison, prepared a box of chocolates, and took them with her to the Beards' residence, where she was due for tea with the doctor's wife.

Mrs. Beard unsuspectingly accepted one of the creams, but the moment she tasted it she spat it out. A doctor's wife may be relied upon to know more than the average woman about poisons, and Mrs. Beard, while contenting herself while Miss Edmunds was with her with a severe criticism of the quality of the chocolates she had bought, later told her husband sufficient to convince him that an attempt had been made on her life.

Dr. Beard wished to prevent a scandal, and he merely informed Miss Edmunds that she must not come to his house again. He refused to attend her any longer, and, in short, proposed to retire out of her life altogether. But he occupied too prominent a position in the heart of the brooding, half-mad woman, who was persuaded that there would be no happiness for either of them unless they were married, for her to agree, but was sane enough to see that before she could resume her friendship with the Beards she must first prove that she had not put the poison in the chocolates she had offered Mrs. Beard.

Christiana Edmunds again secured a quantity of strychnine, and, accosting a boy in the street, she sent him to a sweet shop to purchase a box of chocolates. When the boy returned to her she pretended to examine the contents of the box. Then she reprimanded him for having bought large chocolates instead of small, and sent him back to the shop to effect the exchange. Of course, she had first doctored the chocolates with strychnine before returning the box to the dealer.

She did this at least three times, and only ceased when the shop assistant, rendered suspicious by the repetition of the story of a lady who wanted the box of chocolates changed, followed one of the lads, and saw Christiana

Edmunds. But no one had the slightest suspicion of the woman's object. Her actions were ascribed to eccentricity, and nothing worse.

But by now this sweet shop contained a large quantity of poisoned chocolates, and the unfortunate proprietor, in utter ignorance of the fact, continued to sell his stock. It was, however, only a question of time for a tragedy to occur, and the ultimate victim was a pretty boy only four years old. He was a visitor, and it was his uncle who bought some sweets from the shop to please him. The little fellow gleefully ate one chocolate, and twenty minutes later was dead. The child's uncle tasted the chocolates, and then communicated with the police, who took samples of the confectioner's stock, and, more strychnine having been found, ordered it to be destroyed.

There was an inquest on Sidney Barker, and a verdict of "Accidental death" was given, and the mystery created more than a local sensation and there seemed to be no chance of solving it.

Christiana Edmunds, however, came to the rescue of the police herself. She was not satisfied with the apparent lull in their activities after the verdict of the coroner's jury. She wanted some one to prosecute the owner of the sweet-shop and thereby provide her with proof of her innocence of any design on Mrs. Beard's life. She wished to be able to point to the proceedings against the confectioner and make Dr. Beard and his wife apologise for their base suspicions when they had understood that she was one of the victims of the Brighton tradesman's poisoned stock.

To achieve her object she wrote a series of anonymous letters to the father of Sidney Barker, each letter urging him to launch proceedings against the shopkeeper. These communications were handed over to the police, the handwriting identified, and Christiana Edmunds' arrest was the inevitable sequel.

The trial took place at the Old Bailey before Baron Martin in the early days of 1872, and Mr. Serjeant Ballantine prosecuted. The only survivor amongst judge and counsel is the veteran K.C., Sir Harry Poland, who was junior counsel for the defence, a defence which was simply a plea of insanity.

The verdict of the jury, " Guilty, but insane," was in accordance with public opinion, and Christiana Edmunds was sent to a criminal lunatic asylum. Many persons, however, agreed with Baron Martin's remark that there was a great deal of method in the woman's madness, though only an insane person would have betrayed herself as she did.

It was said of Baron Martin that he greatly objected to murderers escaping the hangman by a plea of insanity, and if that was true it is all the more remarkable that the trial which caused him most inconvenience, and led to many attacks on him, should have been that of George Victor Townley. Sir Samuel was accused of pandering to the influential friends of the murderer by supporting their theory of insanity, and his name will ever be associated with this case as that of the judge who sentenced Townley to death and then saved him from it.

Townley was the son of rich parents, who lived at Hendham Vale, near Manchester. He was an expert linguist and something of a musician, but he had no occupation, living on an allowance from his father. He is best described as an artistic idler, and when he met Bessie

Goodwin at her uncle's house and fell in love with her his outlook on life changed.

Bessie was only on a brief visit to Dr. Goodwin, her uncle, for she passed the greater part of each year with her grandfather, Captain Goodwin, of Wigwell Grange, a pleasant country residence in Wirksworth, Derbyshire. Captain Goodwin was a justice of the peace, and a popular figure in county society, and his granddaughter was quickly made welcome by all his friends.

She was a pretty girl, winsome and dainty, and Townley, an accomplished young man, wooed and won her, despite the opposition of her relatives. The engagement was ratified, and it was understood that as soon as Townley could obtain a situation which would enable him to support a wife they were to be married —an arrangement which has been tried successfully in tens of thousands of love affairs, and one which usually results in happiness for both parties. Townley, however, was no enthusiast on the subject of regular work, and for a few years the engagement drifted on, the man promising always that something would turn up, quite sure that the girl would wait for him.

Bessie Goodwin never complained. Her life was cheerful, and she was perfectly happy. She was young enough to be in a position to afford a long engagement, but it never dawned upon her that another man might come into her life and displace Townley.

Captain Goodwin, her grandfather, was very hospitable, and visitors to Wigwell Grange were frequent. Amongst them was a young clergyman, who came to the Grange about the time when Bessie's engagement to Townley was four years old. He was handsome, clever, of agreeable manners, and, quite apart from his excellent prospects, had sufficient private means to make him a very eligible *parti*.

By this time Bessie's love for Victor Townley was not nearly as strong as it had been, and a week-end in the society of the clergyman killed it. The two young people were mutually attracted, greatly to old Captain Goodwin's delight—he had always disliked Townley—and it was practically settled right away that Bessie should write to her old lover, obtain his permission to break their engagement, and then marry the young clergyman.

It was excusable in the girl that she should conceal from Townley the existence of the other man. In her letter she said that as there was no prospect of marriage they had better free one another from their promise. Townley replied in terms which indicated that he would never consent. Bessie wrote again, imploring his sympathy, but insisting upon an end of the engagement.

The discarded lover guessed that he had been supplanted by a rival, and he soon heard all about the young clergyman's visit to Wigwell Grange. The thought of a successful rival maddened him. He realised that Bessie meant life and happiness to him, and he wrote her a series of letters, pleading for a meeting so that he might take farewell of her. She refused, and he decided to seek her out, but before he began that journey to Wirksworth he had also made up his mind to kill her. If he could not have Bessie Goodwin for his bride no one else should.

He called unexpectedly at the Grange one afternoon and had a brief interview with the nervous, excited girl, who, afraid lest her grandfather might appear at any moment and quarrel with Townley, induced him to go away with a promise that she would slip out before dinner and see him for a few minutes. Townley went away, and spent the intervening hours wandering up and down the neighbouring lanes.

True to her promise, Bessie came to the appointed meeting-place, and for at least ten minutes the one-time lovers talked. Then Townley, realising that she would have none of him, suddenly stabbed her, and she collapsed with a shriek of terror. However, she managed to rise to her feet and guide her tottering footsteps in the direction of home by feeling the wall with her hands. In this condition she was accosted by a labourer, who endeavoured to assist her, but Bessie collapsing again, the labourer had to wait until he could get some one to help him, as alone he was incapable of carrying her to the Grange.

While he was searching the landscape for some one Townley reappeared, and walked up to the spot where Bessie was lying. Not suspecting who Townley was, the man asked him to look after the young lady whilst he ran for additional helpers.

What were Townley's thoughts as he stood on guard over the unconscious form of the girl who, as he must have known, was dying? His face betrayed no emotion. The men who helped to carry Miss Goodwin home afterwards testified to that. Townley was coolness personified when he formed one of the party that conveyed the girl to her grandfather's house, calmly admitting on the way that he was the criminal who had murdered her, for she died before they reached Wigwell Grange, where her grandfather met the procession as it was entering the grounds.

On December 12th, 1864, George Victor Townley was indicted before Baron Martin at the Derby Winter Assizes for the wilful murder of Elizabeth Goodwin. The social position of the accused and the fact that he was a member of a family well known in Manchester and the North gave the case an interest altogether out of the ordinary, which was further heightened by the romantic story of the engagement between the accused and the murdered girl. Of course, the defence could only try to prove that Townley was insane, but the judge from the outset seemed disinclined to accept this plea, and he insisted upon making the jury understand that even if Townley had always been a lunatic, if it was proved that he deliberately planned to take Miss Goodwin's life, and was aware of what he was doing when he stabbed her, he must be deemed to have been sane at the time, and, therefore, guilty of wilful murder.

This expression of opinion on the judge's part was instrumental in securing a verdict of guilty from the jury, and, in passing sentence of death, Baron Martin said that he fully agreed with their decision, yet it was Martin who was the first to cast doubt on the righteousness of the verdict.

During the agitation caused by the astonishing reprieve of Ronald True the case of George Victor Townley was more than once quoted as a sort of precedent, but Townley's escape from the hangman arose out of a series of incidents which are quite unique in the annals of criminal jurisprudence. It was not only a conflict between the lawyers and the alienists, but a source of controversy amongst the doctors themselves.

The first move was made by the judge, Baron Martin, who immediately addressed the following letter to Sir George Grey, the Home Secretary.

"Nottingham, December 13th, 1863.

"George Victor Townley was convicted yesterday before me at Derby of murder and sentenced to be executed. I have directed a copy of my notes to be made for you, should you desire to have it, but there is a full report of the trial in the newspapers. The conviction was in my opinion right, but Dr. Forbes Winslow and Dr. Gisborne were examined at the trial and both deposed in the strongest manner that the prisoner is now of diseased mind and absolutely insane. I think it right to call your attention at once to the subject, with a view to a correct opinion being formed as to the propriety of his execution."

The Home Secretary read the report of the trial and the judge's notes, and decided that Winslow and Gisborne had been taken a little too seriously by the learned baron, but not willing to rely too much on his own judgment he requested Martin to state if he considered Townley was insane. To this the judge replied.

"Norwich, December 18th, 1863.

"I have received your letter of the 17th instant requesting me to inform Sir George Grey whether the impression produced on my mind by the evidence of the two medical witnesses on the trial of George Victor Townley, coupled with the demeanour of the prisoner, was such as to induce me to believe that the prisoner is now insane, or that there is such reason to believe him so as to call for further enquiry. I cannot say that I have formed any decided opinion upon the point. The demeanour of the prisoner afforded me no means of arriving at one. He sat during the trial with his head depressed; I scarcely once saw his countenance; and he never spoke. I should not be justified in saying that the evidence of Dr. Forbes Winslow and Dr. Gisborne is not correct, but I certainly think and have thought ever since the trial, that there ought to be further enquiry.

"I enclose a copy of my notes of the evidence."

Sir George Grey now had recourse to the Lunacy Commissioners, but their report merely added to his difficulties. They declared Townley mentally unsound but responsible for his actions, because while they had no doubt he was at present insane they believed he had been sane enough at the time of the murder. Sir George, on reading this, was disinclined to cancel the execution, which was fixed for December 31st, two days later, but amongst his correspondence he found a document which solved the problem. It was signed by three magistrates and two doctors, and was addressed from the gaol at Derby where Townley was incarcerated, and as it was the subject of world-wide criticism I quote it in full.

"We, the undersigned William Thomas Cox, Thomas Boden Forman, and Thomas Roe, being three justices of the peace for the county and borough of Derby, hereby certify that we this day attended at the county and borough gaol, Derby, and with the aid of Henry Goode, of Derby, aforesaid, doctor of medicine, and Thomas Harwood, of the same place, surgeon, then and there proceeded to examine and inquire into the mental state and condition of George Victor Townley, confined in the said gaol under sentence of death; and we, the said William Thomas Cox, Thomas Boden Forman, Thomas Roe, Henry Goode and Thomas Harwood, further certify that the said George Victor Townley is insane."

Acting on this, the Home Secretary reprieved the murderer, and a great public protest was the immediate result. Letters poured into newspaper offices and leading articles supported their bitter criticisms of the Government. A comparison of the arguments advanced in 1863 and 1922 reveal a wonderful similarity. It was said that Townley had been saved from the scaffold because he had rich and influential relatives; correspondents were eager to be informed why a more obscure murderer of doubtful mentality had not been reprieved; others pointed out that murder would increase if reprieves were easily obtained; and another source of dissatisfaction was the discovery that it was Townley's attorney who had persuaded the Derby magistrates to make an investigation on their own. Finally, it was pointed out that the certificate submitted by the latter gentlemen was not quite in order. To allay public unrest the Home Secretary directed four eminent authorities on mental diseases to examine Townley, and their report was the climax to a sensational affair, the quartette of experts certifying that the prisoner was sane. The question now arose as to what was to be done with Townley. It was within the right of the Government to hang him, but sentiment and precedent alike were against this, and the convict was sent to a penal establishment for life. He did not, however, trouble the prison authorities long. Less than fifteen months subsequent to his reprieve he committed suicide in Pentonville Prison by throwing himself from the top of the circular gallery to the stone floor beneath.

A few years before the Townley sensation Baron Martin was the judge at a trial which may be said to have resembled slightly the circumstances attending the death of Bessie Goodwin. In this instance, however, the accused was a labourer, and his victim a fifteen-year-old servant girl, but love and jealousy were the motives for the crime, and had Frederick Prentice been in a better station of life a very strong case for insanity might have been made out on his behalf.

Emma Coppin was very young, but she was well developed for her age and better educated than her companions. Her father was a labourer, and the family lived at Queenborough, a picturesque Kentish village. Prentice, a powerfully-built youth, in the employment of a farmer, wanted Emma to "walk out" with him, but she refused, not caring for his society, and evidently aiming at something better than the lot of a labourer's wife. However, Prentice was not to be kept at a distance, and as Emma was employed in the Rose Inn it was easy for the young man to see her. He had only to enter and order a glass of beer to have the right to remain in the inn until closing time. Whilst Prentice's friends made fun of his attachment to the girl, he grew more and more determined to have her, or, if he failed in that, to make sure that no one else should.

Emma, who resented his attentions, heard of his threats, but she never suspected that her life was in danger. She was seldom alone, and, besides, she felt that Prentice would not bring himself within reach of the hangman. But Prentice's love for her had affected his brain, and one night when Emma was going home he followed her from the inn and cut her throat with his razor, and left the weapon to be found with the body.

On being arrested he denied nothing, and he told Baron Martin at his trial that he had no excuse to offer, adding that as he had taken away the girl's life he was quite prepared to give his own in return.

When in the condemned cell awaiting his day of doom, Prentice's calm demeanour proved that he was not sane, but he had no influential friends or relatives, and there was no one to step in between him and the executioner. He went to his death without a tremor, expressing himself as pleased with the prospect of leaving this world now that Emma Coppin was no longer in it.

Of the many other trials over which Sir Samuel presided mention should be made of the trial of Tester, Pierce, and Burgess, the three men who stole twelve thousand pounds in gold from the guard's van of a South-Eastern train.

It was a sensational affair, and had there been any honour amongst the thieves the mystery which puzzled the police for eighteen months would never have been solved. But a fourth member of the gang, Agar, who had been sentenced for another offence, discovered that his former comrades were cheating a girl whom he had left in their care, having given Pierce several thousand pounds to pay to her. The girl told Agar, and he retaliated upon his late partners by denouncing them to the police.

Baron Martin sent Tester and Burgess to penal servitude for fourteen years, while Pierce, who was "the head and front of the offending," got two years' hard labour only. The reason for this was that the former were railway servants, and, therefore, liable to heavier penalties. The punishment awarded to Pierce was the maximum.

William James Robson, the clerk who defrauded his employers, the Crystal Palace Company, out of twenty-seven thousand pounds, was tried by Martin, assisted by Mr. Justice Erle, and the thief was given fourteen years.

Another remarkable swindler who appeared before Baron Martin, though only as a witness, was William Roupell, M.P. At the Guildford Assizes on the 18th of August, 1862, Richard Roupell brought an action seeking to eject a Mr. Waite from estates which he, the plaintiff, declared to be his sole property. Mr. Waite had paid hard cash for them to Richard's eldest brother, the well-known M.P., and he declared that the action was a barefaced attempt to deprive him of his rights.

To the surprise of everybody in court William Roupell, who had fled to Spain, to avoid arrest, suddenly appeared, and in the witness-box swore that he had disposed of his brother's property by fraud. It was this confession that led to Roupell's conviction in the following September at the Old Bailey.

So far as the action, Roupell *v.* Waite, was concerned, Baron Martin ordered a juror to be withdrawn, and the contending parties settled their dispute by agreeing to divide the property in question.

Baron Martin's career on the Bench ended in 1874, when he had served twenty-four years. He was made a member of the Privy Council, but for the remaining nine years of his life was seldom seen in public, and he died in 1883 at the age of eighty-two. Sir Samuel, the son-in-law of Sir Frederick Pollock, saw his only child married to another brilliant judge, the late Lord Macnaughten.

Though his judicial duties often brought him

into contact with the worst side of human nature, Sir Samuel never lost his faith in humanity, and he proved himself a wise friend to many persons who had the honour of his acquaintance.

He was often consulted by friends, and his usual advice was: "Don't go to law if you can possibly avoid it." And he spoke as an expert.

CHAPTER XII

Lord Bramwell

George William Bramwell spent thirty-six years administering the law. During his exceptionally long career on the Bench he presided over hundreds of trials, and no judge ever provoked less criticism or gave more satisfaction to the public.

He was a man of great strength of mind, and in his anxiety to save time when counsel were wasting it he would occasionally reveal that irritability of temper which had been one of his chief characteristics at the Bar. But on the whole Bramwell controlled himself and suffered fools gladly.

Born in London, the son of a prosperous banker, Bramwell had a first-class education before beginning his studies for the Bar, to which he was called in 1838. Thirteen years later he was created a Q.C., and in 1856 he was raised to the Bench, being appointed a Baron of Exchequer and knighted. As Baron Bramwell he was known for many years, until 1882, when he was given a peerage and took his seat in the House of Lords as Lord Bramwell of Hever, and he adorned the highest Court of Appeal until his death.

Judges ought to be surprised at nothing and to realise that the criminal mind is capable of the most absurd follies, but on one occasion when reviewing the principal events of his career Lord Bramwell expressed his wonderment at the paltry motive for the crime for which Henry Leigh was hanged in Chester gaol in the late summer of 1877.

Leigh was a young weaver, married, and the father of one child, and he lived in Macclesfield. He was known as a loafer, who was fonder of public-houses than of work, but he never gave any sign that he was a potential murderer. Amongst the friends he and his wife had was a Mrs. Halton, a hard-working widow, who had a daughter eight years old to support. She lived at Sutton, a village just outside the town, and she was on the pay roll of Bamford's factory. One Friday afternoon—March 23rd, 1877, to be exact—Mrs. Halton visited Mrs. Leigh at her home in Fence Street, and soon after her arrival Henry Leigh came in. It was then that Mrs. Halton remarked casually that she would be unable to call at Bamford's for her wages the following morning, and intended to send her little girl for the amount due to her. It was only twelve shillings and threepence, but, of course, of the utmost importance to her. Leigh was greatly interested in the widow's words. He had done no work that week, spending the days loafing about, but his wife knew nothing of this, and she supposed that he, too, would have to receive money from his employer on the usual pay day. Now, Leigh had no desire to confess to her the truth, and, remembering what Mrs. Halton had said, he decided to get possession of that twelve shillings and threepence to save himself from having to admit that he was a dissipated idler.

We have it on Leigh's own authority that he spent most of that night planning how to swindle the widow out of her earnings, but it was not until he had "refreshed" himself at a neighbouring public-house after breakfast that he came to a decision, and that was to turn forger. He wrote a letter purporting to be in Mrs. Halton's handwriting, requesting the manager of Bamford's to hand the bearer her week's money. This note Leigh gave to a boy to take to the factory, but a hitch occurred here, the manager having his suspicions aroused by the wording of the note and declining to act upon it. When the boy returned and reported failure, Leigh coarsely expressed his disappointment and shuffled away.

But he meant to have that twelve shillings and threepence, even if it involved the murder of a human being. He recollected that at a certain time little Mary Ann Halton would toddle into the factory, receive the money, and then start her two and a half miles walk back to her mother's cottage. For the sake of a small sum of money he determined to waylay Mary Ann Halton, rob her, and then throw her into the canal.

Baron Bramwell could hardly believe it possible that a man could have been tempted to plan a murder for so small a sum. It was not a case of sudden temptation, or of spontaneous ferocity inspired by drink. Leigh had not had time to get drunk that day, even had he possessed the means, and he was quite sober when he lay in wait for the child.

He saw her leave the factory, and he invited her to make the journey home along the banks of the canal. Mary Ann knew him as a friend of her mother's, and she scarcely offered any objection. For a few minutes they walked on, Leigh merely waiting until he came to a deserted spot. Then he half-strangled the girl, stole the money—which the child had wrapped up in a handkerchief and placed in a pocket inside her dress—and flung her into the canal.

All for the sake of twelve shillings and threepence! The crime was characterised by great deliberation, but not cunning, for Leigh, had he paused to think, could not have expected to escape justice.

Within an hour of the murder he was drinking in the taproom of the "Old Ship" public-house, and was listening unmoved to the landlady's comments on his dishevelled appearance. But when he had satisfied his thirst he proceeded to his home and handed his wife eight shillings.

They were having their dinner when Mrs. Halton, greatly distressed and excited, entered, and asked Leigh where her child was. It was remarkable that the widow should have thought only of Leigh as the responsible person as soon as she began to be anxious about her little girl. The murderer, of course, denied any knowledge of her whereabouts, but Mrs. Halton, believing that it was either Leigh or nobody, went to the police, and not long afterwards he was arrested.

Whilst awaiting trial he attempted to take his own life by hanging, but he was cut down in time, and lived to hear Baron Bramwell sentence him to death.

A year after the Macclesfield murder the judge tried Joseph Garcia, the Spanish sailor, who murdered five persons at Llangibby, a Monmouthshire village between Newport and Usk. It was practically a massacre, and the motive was robbery.

William Watkins was a farm labourer, who

resided with his wife and three young children in a small cottage that stood in an isolated position. It was its loneliness that attracted the attention of Garcia, who had only just been released from gaol at Usk, and who, sauntering aimlessly down the road that led to Newport, caught sight of the Watkins' cottage and decided that it would be worth entering and robbing.

It was in the month of July, and the day was a long one, but at nine o'clock Garcia crept over the fields and entered the cottage, for the front door was open. Watkins happened to be in the little garden, and Garcia could see him from the window. The scoundrel hesitated for a few seconds, realising that at any moment Watkins might return and discover him. He wanted to rob the cottage at his leisure, and, therefore, he crept back into the garden, came close behind Watkins, and with one blow stunned him and cut the unfortunate man's throat. He had just finished when Mrs. Watkins hurried out. Probably she had heard her husband fall and was anxious about him. But she did not live long enough after seeing Garcia to utter a cry for help. He was quickly upon her, and she was soon lying dead at his feet.

Leaving the bodies of his victims lying on the ground, the murderer hastened into the cottage and ran upstairs. The three Watkins' children were, of course, in bed, and the bloodthirsty ruffian, who could easily have taken what he wanted without disturbing them, calmly proceeded to murder all three. Then, at last, satiated with blood, he proceeded to search for goods and money. There was very little cash, but he found Watkins' best suit, and decided that it would do for him, and, adding to it a collection of clothes, he escaped from the house and made his way across country.

The discovery of the five-fold crime horrified the countryside, and had any of the unofficial "policemen" found Garcia they would have lynched him there and then. The Watkins had been highly respected, and their savage destruction roused in the breast of every decent man a desire to avenge them personally.

But a policeman saved Garcia from "Judge Lynch" by arresting him about twenty-four hours after the murder, and as he was actually wearing poor Watkins' best suit and his much-mended best boots the villain's protests of innocence could not be treated seriously. But other evidence was secured, amongst the witnesses being two who identified Garcia as the foreign-looking man they had seen near the Watkins' cottage on the fatal day.

When the defence applied for the trial to be transferred to another district the application was immediately granted. No one challenged the decision. It was common knowledge that every time Garcia had appeared at the police court at Caerleon he had run the risk of being lynched by the crowd. He was hooted and threatened, and he retorted by making faces and screaming curses. It was therefore just as well that he should be brought up at the Gloucester Assizes, and before Baron Bramwell, who could be relied upon to pay attention to the evidence only.

One can, of course, sympathise with the country folk who in their rough way wished to settle the matter there and then. Garcia had no defence except a blank denial, but the character of British justice had to be maintained, even if it meant spending a lot of money over as depraved a murderer as the world has ever known.

In a few telling sentences the judge expressed his agreement with the verdict of the jury, and in solemn tones condemned the Spaniard to be hanged. Garcia listened unmoved, and even the howls of the mob outside the court failed to affect him. He bowed ironically to Baron Bramwell, and with a smile disappeared, joking with the police when they bundled him into the prison van, and laughing uproariously when a crowd several thousands strong made a last effort to get hold of him. It was generally agreed that this wholesale murderer possessed an iron nerve that nothing, however fearful, could disturb, but the truth was that he had only been acting.

Like all callous murderers, he was an arrant coward at heart. The man who had sent five persons to a sudden death was terrified at the prospect of facing eternity himself. He passed the night before his execution whining for mercy, and when Marwood came to prepare him for his end the fellow seemed half-dead already. Terror had nearly deprived him of the use of his limbs, and his eyes appeared to be leaving their sockets. But he would not confess, and he went into the next world with a lie on his lips.

The story of the *Flowery Land* pirates is one of those romances of the sea which imitate fiction very closely. It might have been invented by Robert Louis Stevenson or Captain Marryat, but it was a dreadful reality, and it was Baron Bramwell who heard it in full at the Old Bailey sixty years ago.

On July 28th, 1863, the *Flowery Land* left London for Singapore. It was commanded by Captain John Smith, who had two mates to assist him, and of the fourteen seamen eight were foreigners. From all accounts the foreign seamen began to complain soon after the ship had receded out of sight of land, but owing to the captain's conciliatory rule nothing happened until the morning of September 10th. Then at three o'clock the chief mate, who was on watch, was suddenly attacked by half a dozen men, who beat him about the head and finished him off with knives.

The noise of the affray roused the captain, who rushed from his cabin, but he was instantly confronted by the mutineers and hacked to pieces, and the captain's brother—the only passenger—was also murdered by being thrown into the sea. Afterwards they attacked the second mate, but he escaped to his cabin, locked himself in, and managed to keep them at bay until they had time to realise that he was the only man left who could navigate the vessel, none of the mutineers being capable of performing that essential duty. But the mate knew that his life was daily in danger, and he suffered agonies through his dread of sleep, fearing that at any moment he might meet with the same fate as the captain if he closed his eyes.

Taffer, the second mate, brought the *Flowery Land* to the mouth of the River Plate, a hundred and sixty miles from Monte Video, the capital of Uruguay. His troubles were not ended even now, for the mutineers decided to scuttle the ship, and to safeguard their own miserable lives resolved on the murder of the mate, the steward, the lamp-trimmer, and the cook—all British subjects.

The four were actually in a boat and about to row away from the doomed ship, when they were brought back, and the steward flung overboard. The mate was ordered into another boat, while the lamp-trimmer and the cook were left to drown in the sinking ship.

The mate acted as spokesman for the band of mutineers when their boat reached land, and as two of them were always close behind him with daggers in their hands he did not hesitate to repeat the agreed lie that they were shipwrecked mariners, giving the name of a fictitious vessel in corroboration. However, Taffer was determined that the murderers should not escape, and at the first opportunity he told the truth, and, with the help of a friendly Englishman, got the local authorities to move.

The mutineers were captured and brought before a naval court, and, after an inquiry, sent back to England in irons.

The case against them was so clear that the defence—a complaint of ill-treatment on the captain's part—seemed ludicrously feeble, and counsel for the pirates had an unenviable task. As Baron Bramwell pointed out, no harshness on the captain's part could have justified a wholesale massacre, and it was not suggested even by the ruffians that the lamp-trimmer, for example, was deserving of death because the captain did not provide the seamen with proper food.

Seven out of the eight prisoners were found guilty, and the Home Secretary reprieving two —the youngest of the conspirators—five of the *Flowery Land* pirates were publicly executed in the presence of a crowd that exceeded one hundred thousand persons, who were guilty of excesses which ought to have caused the authorities there and then to abolish public executions. But it was five years ere that much-needed reform was carried out.

The Cannon Street murder, one of the most sensational events of the year 1866, still puzzles the criminologists, and never in the history of crime has a murder trial produced more circumstantial evidence and less proof. At one time it seemed as though the accused man must be convicted, and yet, after a remarkably able speech for the prosecution, the defence triumphed, and the prisoner left the dock a free man.

The details of the crime are many and interesting, but I will summarise them as briefly as possible. Mrs. Sarah Milson was housekeeper to Messrs. Bevington and Sons, of 2, Cannon Street, London, and at the end of each day's work, when the staff had departed and the premises locked up, Mrs. Milson and the cook remained alone in the building. The two women became close friends, but the cook soon had reason to believe that Mrs. Milson had a "secret," for several times a man called after dark, and the housekeeper always gave him money. Usually she returned from the interview at the street door in a state of half-suppressed agitation.

A few days before the crime took place Mrs. Milson borrowed two sovereigns from her to hand over to the mysterious caller, and when one night, about nine, the bell rang, and Mrs. Milson called out that it was for her, and that she would answer it, cook, guessing that it was the mysterious man again, did not stir.

She merely waited in her room, and when the "interview" was prolonged was hardly surprised. At last, however, she became impatient, and lighting a candle she proceeded downstairs. At the bottom of the stairs she came upon the corpse of her friend. Mrs. Milson's last interview with the blackmailer had resulted in her brutal murder.

The detective force set to work at once, and quickly discovered the identity of the man who had received several pounds from the unfortunate woman. Some threatening letters which talked of exposing her to her employers were produced, and these were proved to be in the handwriting of William Smith, an Eton resident. He was arrested, and the whole of his relations with Mrs. Milson came out.

It was a peculiar story he told. The housekeeper had borrowed money from a Mrs. Webber, a man of the name of George Terry apparently acting as security. Terry eventually went into the workhouse, but Mrs. Milson was in his debt on account of the loan, and Terry, making the acquaintance of William Smith, the latter agreed to act as a go-between and recover the debt from Mrs. Milson on his behalf. Smith therefore called at Cannon Street, and received two pounds from the housekeeper, but unknown to Terry he called on other occasions and was paid small sums, which he kept for himself.

It was obvious, therefore, that William Smith did play an important part in the closing month of Sarah Milson's life, but it seemed impossible that he should have murdered her on her own doorstep, for there was a complete absence of motive, though, as a great judge had laid down, there is no obligation to prove motive to convict a person charged with murder.

Smith was identified by a woman as having been in Cannon Street the day before the murder, and altogether counsel for the prosecution made out a very strong case, based entirely, of course, on circumstantial evidence.

The defence was an alibi, and never was an alibi more clearly proved. Witness after witness entered the box and swore that William Smith had been in Eton at the very time Sarah Milson was murdered in Cannon Street. Beginning at an early hour in the afternoon of the day of the crime, the accused's movements were traced right up to midnight, and during that time he had certainly not been outside Eton. After that there was no doubt as to what the verdict of the jury would be.

Baron Bramwell's summing up was admirable and to the point. He was an acknowledged authority on the law of evidence, and his impartiality and sound judgment did more than influence the jury to acquit the prisoner. They helped to convince the general public that no matter how strong may be their desire to avenge the dead, they must first of all be just to the living.

For many a long day after Smith's acquittal the Cannon Street murder continued to exercise the minds of the best detectives, but no one else was ever arrested, and the case remains amongst the great mysteries of crime for all time.

About forty years ago a prize fight took place between two men, Young and Wilmot, in a house in the neighbourhood of the Haymarket, London. The audience was a small and select one, being composed of young bloods and leaders of "the fancy." The two men battered away at one another until Wilmot, covered with bruises, collapsed, and the fight was awarded to Young. But those present were alarmed when they could not restore Wilmot to consciousness, and he was immediately carried to Charing Cross Hospital, where he died a few hours later.

The survivor of the contest and several of the spectators were arrested and charged with manslaughter, and when the case came before Baron Bramwell at the Old Bailey it excited enormous interest, because on the judge's decision rested the future of the art of fisticuffs. Were the accused found guilty of manslaughter, it would mean that any spectator of a similar contest would, in the event of an accident happening and any of the combatants dying, be liable to a criminal charge.

Bramwell had a difficult task. Public opinion was dead against the boxing fraternity, which in those days was ninety per cent. riff-raff and ten per cent. silly youths with more money than brains. Every disreputable public-house had its "ring," and the "sport" was in a terrible state, "faked matches" being very common.

However, Bramwell was not to be biased. The evidence proved that this particular fight had been "on the square," and that the rules of boxing had been scrupulously observed; so, while letting the "pugs" and their friends understand that he regarded the "sport" with no great favour, he advised the jury to return a verdict of "not guilty," and boxing escaped a premature death.

There was one prisoner who might have avoided the hangman had not Baron Bramwell been too kind to her. This was Catherine Wilson, the poisoner. She was brought before him on a charge of having attempted to poison Sarah

Cornell, and, despite evidence which nowadays reads quite sufficient to convict, the learned judge found a weak point in the prosecution, and, out of pity for the friendless woman in the dock, made the most of it. He summed up in her favour, and the jury acquitted.

Catherine Wilson triumphantly left the dock, her face beaming, and congratulating herself on being the cleverest woman in the world to have outwitted judge and jury alike. But she would have cursed his lordship's impartiality had she known that there was a detective in court with a warrant for her arrest on a charge of murder, and that he had been instructed to leave her alone if the jury sent her to penal servitude. Catherine Wilson was, therefore, arrested, and a few months later was executed for her diabolical crimes.

In the late 'sixties there was a great deal of mischievous activity on the part of the Fenians, and Baron Bramwell was engaged in two trials which helped to stamp out that dangerous secret society. He was with Lord Chief Justice Cockburn when Michael Barrett was condemned for the Clerkenwell outrage, which caused several deaths, and he was the presiding judge at the trial of three men—Berry, Casey, and Shaw—who were indicted for conspiracy against the Crown.

There was not a little unconscious humour in this trial, for it was proved that the three men, almost wholly illiterate and penniless, attempted to found an organisation in England with the object of seizing arms—Chester Castle was to have been stormed and the arms and ammunition there captured for the benefit of the Fenians.

The programme did not err on the side of timidity, and had not the Fenians been responsible for so many outrages it is likely that these three men would not have been taken as seriously as they were. However, the majesty of the law was upheld, and Baron Bramwell, an admirable judge for cases of this sort, sent Berry to penal servitude for fifteen years, while Shaw was given seven. Casey managed to secure an acquittal and quickly made himself scarce.

It should be mentioned that it was with the object of rescuing these three men from the clutches of the law that Michael Barrett and his confederates committed the Clerkenwell outrage. The accused were under remand, and Barrett hoped to free them and get them out of the country before a judge and jury could deal with them.

The Fenians were a miserable lot, and whenever they were guilty of violence and the police were on their track nearly every man jack of them wanted to turn queen's evidence and betray his fellows.

On one occasion when the authorities suspected five men of having attempted to dynamite a judge's house they were embarrassed when six men called at various police stations, each anxious to "inform" against his comrades. It was this competition to turn traitor that really finished the Fenians. They could not trust one another, and in sheer terror they disbanded.

An action brought by a well-known Kensington resident against the Sun Insurance Company at the Croydon Assizes in the early 'sixties created tremendous interest in society circles.

Campden House, Kensington, was a substantial residence, in the occupation of Mr. and

Mrs. Woolley, who entertained largely, specialising in poets and artists, and by their hospitality earning a reputation for geniality and wealth. Mr. Woolley was an invalid, and as he valued the contents of his home at thirty thousand pounds he insured it for that sum, dividing the amount amongst half a dozen companies. It was a large sum, but Campden House was said to be filled with treasures, for which reason it was the favourite resort of those happy beings who possessed the artistic temperament.

One night a fire broke out in Campden House and totally destroyed it, and Mr. Woolley promptly notified the insurance companies, and inspectors were sent to examine the ruins. They reported that the house had been insured beyond its value, and, furthermore, that Mr. Woolley was no invalid at all, but a healthy man who had posed as a sufferer for years, having really planned the fire long before it took place.

It was a serious accusation, and Mr. Woolley brought a suit against the "Sun," and on the result of this action the other companies decided to stand.

Baron Bramwell presided, and a jury of intelligent men heard the evidence for and against. Everything depended on Mr. Woolley, who entered the witness-box with the heavy deliberation of a confirmed invalid, and, although subjected to a severe cross-examination, gained the sympathy of the jury.

The counsel for the Sun Insurance Company could not overcome the impression the plaintiff had made, and the jury saved his name and reputation, and, incidentally, gained for him the thirty thousand pounds for which he had come down upon the insurance companies.

When, in 1882, Bramwell was raised to the peerage, his place henceforth was with the Law Lords, and in that calm atmosphere he passed the remaining years of his life, years of repose after the strenuous labours of criminal courts in London and the provinces.

THE END

INDEX

Printed in Great Britain at the Richmond Hill Printing Works, Ltd.——Bournemouth